THE ALTERNATIVE GCSE GUIDES

ENGLISH
LANGUAGE

EXAM SUCCESS WITHOUT THE STRESS

Sherry Ashworth
Illustrated by Polly Dunbar

SCHOLASTIC

To Emma Unsworth.

Sherry Ashworth is an English teacher, freelance journalist and writer of fiction for teenagers. She lives in Manchester with her husband and two daughters.

With thanks to our educational consultants, Anna Johnson and Sarah Golding.

Scholastic Children's Books,
Commonwealth House, 1-19 New Oxford Street,
London, WC1A 1NU, UK
A division of Scholastic Ltd
London - New York - Toronto - Sydney - Auckland
Mexico City - New Delhi - Hong Kong

First published in the UK by Scholastic Ltd, 2001

The extract on page 78 is reproduced by kind permission of Sam Hart and *The Big Issue*.

ISBN 0 439 01267 8

Typeset by M Rules
Printed by Cox & Wyman Ltd, Reading, Berks.

10 9 8 7 6 5 4 3 2 1

Contents

Hello. . .

Are you looking for help with your English GCSE? Maybe you're just about to start the course and feel confused?

> Too right! All the different stuff I have to write does my head in.

Or maybe you need help with your coursework. . . Or you want to improve your predicted grade?

> That won't be difficult...

Or the exam is too close for comfort... Or you've never sussed out what your English teachers really want from you?

Or English is bugging you, and you want to enjoy it again?

Or you think you're OK at English, but you'd like to get better?

I think you've come to the right place – the only alternative GCSE guide that guarantees you a few laughs as well as results.

This book is most definitely *not* a textbook. Would you really want to read a textbook from cover to cover? I think not. This book dishes the dirt on what the examiners *really* want (apart from all June and July in the Bahamas), your English teacher's quirks, and short cuts to getting good grades. English is actually a lot easier than you think – I mean, you use it every day, don't you?

So put your feet up, get a king-size bar of chocolate, and read the book through now.

That'll give you an idea of which sections are most useful to you – everyone's different. Then you can home in on the parts that you need, and start applying those tips right away. Your English teacher will be bound to notice the difference.

One more thing – you'll have spotted another difference between this alternative guide and your ordinary textbook. This book occasionally uses slang and abbreviations. When *you* write formal English at GCSE level, you're best off avoiding them (see page 149). This isn't a formal textbook, however. It's more like a best mate who tells it like it is, and lets you in on the secret thoughts of the examiner...

Amazing fact! Examiners were once ordinary human beings. Some are even mothers and fathers, and many of them were or are practising English teachers. But once they've been to a few standardisation meetings to learn how to mark scripts, strange changes take place...

*tends to daydream
— try to prevent this*

*fussy about
spelling, grammar
and punctuation*

*worries — are
they awarding
the marks
correctly?*

*loves
candidates
who answer
the questions
exactly as set*

*wants to award
marks and will
with some
encouragement*

tends to overeat

SWEE

PARTY TRICKS

*has difficulty reading
messy handwriting*

gets bored easily

8

A list of things which will not impress your examiner

1. A ten-pound note folded into your script.

2. Coursework folders with coffee-stains.

3. A threat to come round to their place and duff them up if they don't give you an A*.

4. Not reading the questions properly.

5. Commenting that you're off on holiday now while they've got to stay at home marking.

6. Handwriting that even Sherlock Holmes couldn't decipher.

7. Mistakes in spelling and grammar.

8. Doodles in the margin – you mean you have time to doodle?

Watch out for more revelations and secret thoughts of the examiner... but meanwhile, relax. Remember, English should be the most fun subject on any school's curriculum.

Why's that, then?

Where shall I start? In all the other subjects, there's a mass of learning, but with English Language there's very little actual revision to do. But it's not just that. English is about people, and if you're good at English, especially speaking and listening, it helps you get on with all sorts of people.

Like people you fancy.

Especially people you fancy. Writing English is just as useful. Writing a good letter of complaint will get you your money back, and if you want any kind of job, you'll probably have to write a letter of application. And, if you get really good at it, you can write best-selling novels, or finalize the details on a treaty for world peace. When you're not working you'll want to read books and magazines, and be able to sort through ads to work out who's giving the best deal.

So you need to get your English sorted for whatever you want to be.

Right. But it's not only useful, and it's not just that people tend to notice how well you write and speak. It's dead interesting. You can read newspapers and work out what the writer wants to make you think, get the most out of a good book, and find out about other people and different lifestyles. In English lessons you can have a good argument, and work out where you stand on various issues – your English teacher is keen to know what *you* think. English is your language – it's the most widely spoken in the Western world, it's the main language of the Internet and it's the language of the future. A qualification in English is most definitely one worth having.

First we'd better find out what *your* syllabus is…

What is a syllabus?

A syllabus is examiner-talk meaning "a course of study". It tells you what your coursework folder should include, and roughly what's going to be on your examination papers. It also lets you know the skills you're being tested on. That's why it's a good idea to know what's on your syllabus.

In Great Britain, there are six examination boards, and they all like to be different. (Definitely members of the awkward squad.) First you're going to have to find out which examination board you're sitting. Your teacher will know the answer to this. Just make sure your teacher's bang up to date on the details – the examination boards have a habit of changing the syllabuses every so often. Examiners get bored very, very easily. Perhaps this is why they're called examination boards! (Groan.)

All six syllabuses do have things in common. These are:

- 20 per cent of your marks come from oral assignments, or SPEAKING AND LISTENING (see chapter 6).

- 20 per cent of your marks come from your COURSEWORK folder – pieces of writing composed by you during your course with some guidance from your teacher.

- 60 per cent of your marks come from TWO EXAMS, each of which is around two hours long – check exact times with your board.

- Every board requires you to have read some Shakespeare and other literature as well as factual texts.

- Every board expects you to recognize the difference between fact and opinion.

Also, the boards agree on three groups of skills they're going to look for in students. These are the ability to:

INFORM   **ARGUE**   **ANALYSE**

EXPLAIN   **PERSUADE**   **REVIEW**

DESCRIBE **INSTRUCT** **COMMENT**

Like – erm – run those past me again?

No sweat.

1. INFORM ... EXPLAIN ... DESCRIBE means writing (or speaking) in a straightforward way about something, probably putting information in your own words.

2. ARGUE ... PERSUADE ... INSTRUCT means putting across your point of view in writing (or in a class), so that you're getting someone to do something, or making them think like you do.

3. ANALYSE ... REVIEW ... COMMENT means writing (or speaking) about language in detail and working out exactly what it's telling you, and whether it's good at telling you what it's telling you – that is, how effective it is.

15

So I have to put stuff in my own words, persuade people and then weigh up detail...

You've got it. The rest of this book will show you how to improve these skills.

OK. I'm fine with that. But this coursework and exam business. I don't get it. Which one is more important? Why do we have to have both? If I don't do the coursework, will I still pass?

Hold on. There are three questions there.

- You have to do both because it's fairer. Some people do better under exam conditions and others do better when they can spend longer on their work. Also coursework and exams demand different skills.

- Both are important, but you get more marks for your exam.

- If you don't do the coursework, you'll get a much lower grade than you would otherwise. You'd be 20 per cent worse off to start with. Doing a good coursework folder gives you a head start.

I'd better get going on my coursework folder.

Then turn to page 202 and read the section on coursework. Here's a list of things you might be expected to do either for coursework or in the exam in GCSE English. Tick off the ones that apply to you. If you're not sure which ones to do, check with your teacher:

☐ answer questions on a passage taken from a newspaper, magazine, advertisement, leaflet or other factual source (p.53)

☐ compare and contrast passages (p.91)

☐ write creatively, i.e. write a story (p.139)

☐ write something personal about yourself (p.153)

☐ write an imaginary magazine or newspaper article, or leaflet, flyer, review, etc. (p.131)

☐ write a letter (p.126)

☐ answer questions on a passage of literature you haven't seen before (p.93)

☐ use an anthology of texts and study them before the exam, then write about them (p.100)

☐ study Shakespeare (p.101)

☐ write something expressing your point of view (p.134)

☐ explain something (p.128)

When you've ticked this list, use the page numbers to look up the relevant sections in the book. But don't ignore the other sections – you might miss something that could make all the difference to you.

Even basics drive me batty!

Spelling

Oh, no! Not spelling again. Ever since I was a kid, I've been nagged about my spelling. Why does it matter? Everyone knows what I'm on about even if I get letters round the wrong way.

Readers might know what you mean, but inaccurate spelling can give the impression that you don't care, and your mistakes can be distracting. Many people (including examiners and potential employers) are likely to think the worst of candidates with poor spelling.

OK, I could try a little harder, I suppose. But there are some words I'll never be able to spell.

You don't have to be perfect, but do try to tidy up your act as much as you can. And take heart – some very clever and well-educated people have appalling spelling. People who are naturally good at spelling are lucky; the rest of us suffer from occasional word-blindness. Generally people with the knack for spelling have a good visual memory. Even if you don't, there are still things you can do to improve matters – and it's worth doing!

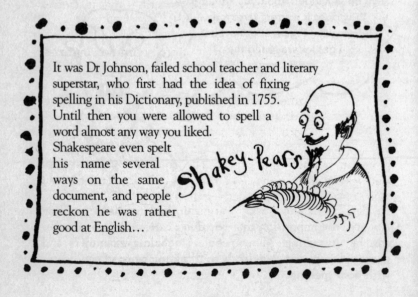

It was Dr Johnson, failed school teacher and literary superstar, who first had the idea of fixing spelling in his Dictionary, published in 1755. Until then you were allowed to spell a word almost any way you liked. Shakespeare even spelt his name several ways on the same document, and people reckon he was rather good at English...

Shakey-Pears

Spelling tip one – break 'em up

If there are words that you find hard to spell, break them up into segments and learn the segments. Learning spellings in this way can even help you suss out their meaning.

For example, *unconscious* is a pain to learn. Try learning instead *un* + *con* + *sci* + *ous*.

> **un = a negative, not**
> **con = has the rough meaning of "with"**
> **sci = always has something to do with knowing**
> **ous = has an adjectival or describing function**

So unconscious means *in a state of being without knowledge,* or not knowing what is going on (passed out).

If you become an expert at this way of learning spellings, you might begin to notice that most word segments do seem to obey certain rules. One that's worth knowing concerns segments that usually go at the beginning or ends of words – that is, prefixes (the beginnings) and suffixes (the ends).

Some common prefixes	Some common suffixes
to-	-able
mis-	-ous
un-	-less
dis-	-ly
pre-	-ing

You can probably find others. The point about prefixes and suffixes is that when they join on to the basic segment of a word, you don't need to drop or add letters.

Hold on.
You're getting
complicated.

21

OK. Let's look at some examples.

    for + give + ness = forgiveness
    dis + miss + ing = dismissing
    consider + ate = considerate
    un + necessary = unnecessary
    comfort + able = comfortable
    clue + less = clueless

When you form words like these made up of smaller parts (compound words), don't be tempted to add or take away letters.

English is actually one of the most difficult languages to spell correctly, because many of our words are derived from different languages from Anglo-Saxon, Latin and French to Indian languages and American English. So pity the poor non-English speaker who learns English as a foreign language and has to get his or head round all our spellings!

Hey! I've thought of an exception to your rule about prefixes and suffixes. Watch this: "spotty" – a word, right? "er" – a suffix, a segment that comes at the end of the word. BUT – you write "SPOTTIER", don't you? Not "spottyer".

OK. You have found an exception. Unfortunately, English is littered with exceptions. If I was to tell you all the exceptions to spelling rules I'd need to write another book.

Yeah. Like if I want to write "hoping", which is made up of hope + ing, I have to drop the "e". And all + together is spelt "altogether". And care + full is spelt "careful"…

Shut up, will you? I admit there are loads of exceptions, which is why learning spelling rules can be sometimes self-defeating. At GCSE level, when you've already learned the basics of spelling, you're better off improving your spelling by just concentrating on the mistakes *you* generally make.

Spelling tip two – write 'em down

Get a notebook and jot down 50 spelling errors you've made recently. Using a dictionary or someone who's good at spelling like an English teacher, write down the correct versions. Divide your words into segments and then learn five words a day. Test yourself on them every so often. Make a poster of them and stick them on the door of the loo. In ten days you will have improved your spelling dramatically.

How would you pronounce the word "GHOTI"?

Well, you *could* pronounce it "fish": "gh" is pronounced "f" in "cough", "o" is pronounced "ih" in "women" and "ti" is pronounced "sh" in "nation".

GHOTI

Spelling tip three – the sneakiest words

Check you're wise to the most common spelling errors, and learn the correct versions of those. To help you, we've compiled our top 20 commonly mis-spelled words…

AND IN AT NO. 20, NO MOVEMENT FROM LAST WEEK...

20
LIGHTNING

That's right, folks, there's no "E" in lightning with a flash, only in thunder. And a bit of a tear-jerker, the next one...

19
TRAGEDY

If there's only one "D" in disaster, there's only one in tragedy. And at no. 18, moving slowly down the charts...

18
CHARACTER

Only one "H" in second position there. Steady at no. 17 is...

17
ETC (short for etcetera)

No other order is acceptable. Not that you'd use an abbreviation in an essay... Now bon appetit for...

16
RESTAURANT

Where the "A" comes before the "U" – plain alphabetical order in this traditional dining establishment. At 15 is an old favourite...

15
DOESN'T

Begins with "DOE", a female deer. And neck and neck at 14 is the funniest duo since Laurel and Hardy...

14
HUMOUR AND HUMOROUS

Collapse with laughter as that sneaky little second "U" in "HUMOUR" runs out from behind the "R" and tucks itself in behind the "S" in "HUMOROUS". And at 13 we have...

25

13
INDEPENDENT

Apart from the "I" at the beginning, the "E"s like to go it alone.
Stand in line for the chart-busting...

12
QUEUE

That's right — q, you ee, you ee — a simple repetition there.
And you'll find that you can't do without...

11
NECESSARY

One "C", two "S"s followed by an "A". Is necessary the
correct way?

10
DEFINITELY

Remember it's I – N – I in the middle and "ELY" at the end – then
you definitely won't go wrong. Now we're in the top ten, so mind
your own...

9
BUSINESS

I know that "U" and "I" have a fatal attraction, but make sure
they're always separated by the "S". Marching onwards at no. 8
is...

8
SOLDIER

Quake, as you notice there's "DIE" in the middle! And at no. 7?
Don't jump to conclusions – it's...

7
PREJUDICE

Yep, there's only one "D" in prejudice, just before the "ICE",
whichever way you look at it. Look who's at no. 6...

6
SEPARATE
There's an old saying, "PA pays the RATEs". Except a) this is sexist as Ma can pay rates too and b) we don't have rates any more, we have council tax instead. But "Mum pays the council tax by standing order" doesn't have the same ring to it. At no. 5...

5
ACCOMMODATION
This desirable residence comes fully equipped with 2 "C"s, 2 "M"s, 1 "D" and a patio without the "P" and instead an "N" at the end with fine views of the surrounding countryside. At no. 4 we have...

4
PSYCHOLOGIST
The silent "P" leads immediately into "S" – Y? – then a "CH" and you're on your way. And get ready to rap for no. 3...

3
RHYTHM
Got a little rhyme, and it's a gem: R H Y and T H M.
Listen to the beat and say it again: R H Y and T H M.
And at no. 2?

2
DESPERATE
Just like you are, when you struggle to spell this little charmer. But when I tell you that the singer/composer of this jazzy number is Des Perate, it'll all become clear. And top of the charts, for the sixteenth year in succession...

1
EMBARRASSMENT
... the feeling you get when you realize you've spelt it wrong yet again. But worry no longer. Think 2 "R"s for going doubly red and 2 "S"s for feeling doubly stupid.

If your favourite spelling errors haven't charted this week, don't despair. Just make up your own daft way of remembering them – the dafter, the better!

Another common source of spelling errors is words that sound the same but are spelt differently according to their meaning.

Like "source", which could be "sauce" if you pour it on your chips.

That's enough of your sauce! As I was saying, get yourself acquainted with the words that you're most likely to mix up.

GROUP ONE	GROUP TWO	GROUP THREE
There – refers to a place, like "where", or "here"	**Their** – belongs to them	**They're** – short for 'they are' – the clue is the apostrophe
Two – a number, compare with "twelve" and "twenty"	**Too** – also – because you've got an "o" and also another "o"	**To** – a direction word, or an infinitive, very short
Weather – the climate – is it warm enough to <u>eat</u> out?	**Whether** – introduces alternatives – <u>wh</u>ether to use <u>wh</u> is the question	
Principle – law, personal code of conduct – as a <u>rule</u>	**Principal** – the head of an organization… a person… a <u>pal</u> is a person	
Lose – the opposite of find, pronounced *luze*	**Loose** – wobbly, pronounced *loo-ss*	

28

Pick the correct word from one of the three boxes to complete the following conversation.

– Look over th_____! He's cute!
– I fancy his mate, t_____!
– I don't know w_____ we should go up to them or not.
– It's my belief girls should chat up boys. On p_____, I think we should.

– I like th_____ trainers.
– Suitable for any sort of w_____.
– There are t_____ of them and t_____ of us.
– I say we ought to walk over t_____ them.
– I'm scared I'll l_____ my confidence.
– T_____ late. Th_____ walking away!

Answers on page 220.

Sometimes words are spelt differently depending on whether they're nouns or verbs.

Hey!
A noun is a person, place or thing, isn't it?
And a verb is a doing word?

You've got it. Here are a couple of examples of what I mean:

- As a noun PRACTICE ends with CE. (Sit down and do your piano practice!) As a verb PRACTISE ends with SE. (You should practise your spelling.)

- As a noun <u>E</u>FFECT means the change on something. As a verb, <u>A</u>FFECT means to change something. (I affected my exam results by working very hard, which had a pleasing effect on my parents.)

Spelling tip four – memory trick

If there's a word you just can't memorize, try spelling out a crazy phrase from its letters, like these...

REIGN   Rabbits
         Eat
         Interesting
         Green
         Nibbles

PERSUADE Please
         Empty
         Red
         Satchels
         Under
         A
         Dark
         Elephant

And just remember, if you want to use a long or complex word in an exam and you're not sure how to spell it, *use it anyway*. Make an intelligent guess at the spelling, and go for it. Live dangerously! The examiners will forgive you, I promise. No one's perfect. Everyone makes mistakes ~~ocassionaly~~… ~~occassionally~~… ~~ocasionaly~~… occasionally. (Yesss!)

Spelling tip five – keep reading

A very enjoyable way to improve your spelling is to read more. You'll automatically absorb the appearance of unfamiliar words. Try reading anything – fiction, non-fiction – for just half an hour a day, and watch your confidence grow! And even if you can't remember all the correct spellings you meet, you'll begin to recognize when you make mistakes, and recognizing your own mistakes is halfway to improvement.

There are some easy-to-spell pairs of words that seem to have a fatal attraction for one another, and we can't seem to stop ourselves joining them up. Believe it or not (and you'd better believe it!) "a" and "lot" are *two separate words*. Look at the list below – all of these pairs must stay separate.

a	lot
in	front
thank	you
as	well
in	fact

Fifty years ago "alright" could only be spelt as "all right". The English language is constantly changing, however, and nowadays it is acceptable to write "alright" – you can thank the Americans for that!

Another all-too-common spelling error occurs with the verbs *could*, *would* and *should*. Sometimes they need the extra helping verb "have" to show they are in the past tense. Look at these examples.

> **I could have eaten all of the cow pie.**
> **I should have looked where I was going.**
> **I would have liked to have gone to the concert.**

Abbreviated, in written dialogue, you could write:

> **I could've eaten...**
> **I should've looked...**
> **I would've liked...**

The sound "'ve" sounds very much like "of" and some people use the word "of" instead of "have". This is wrong.

Well, you could have knocked me down with a feather. I've been using "of" for years.

Glad you've learnt something!

Spelling tip six – final check
Most people can spell reasonably well if they have time, a dictionary in front of them, and a parent in the kitchen or a teacher in the classroom. However, most of us go to ~~peises~~ ... ~~peaces~~ ... pieces in exams, when we're rushed and under stress. Unfortunately, it's our exam papers that the examiner gets to see.

So it's a really good idea to build in time when you're writing your exam paper to look through your spellings. Make sure you learn the words you usually get wrong, check to see if you've used them, and correct them. Reading through your work is always advisable in exams, and it gives you a chance to tweak your spellings into shape.

Punctuation

Sounds like you could do with a visit to…

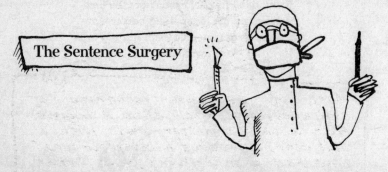

The Sentence Surgery

PATIENT –
Good morning, Doctor you have a nice surgery my problem is easy to describe when I get work back from my teacher I see spots all over the page.

DOCTOR –
You either have a liver infection or she's adding the full stops that you should have put in it.

PATIENT –
Can I die from not using full stops properly?

DOCTOR –
It could be fatal in a GCSE exam.

PATIENT –
Aaargh!

GOVERNMENT HEALTH WARNING

Commas should not be used for adding sentences to other sentences, or as substitutes for full stops.

A doctor writes:

> Most of us can recognize a sentence, and know that it begins with a capital letter, ends with a full stop, expresses a complete idea, and has a main verb in it. What many people fail to understand is that a sentence may be very short. For example: "It rains." "The door opened." Instead of ending with a full stop, they use a comma, despite the government health warning. Other people write at such speed that they forget to use full stops. This is not a symptom of genius but carelessness.

DOCTOR –

Now repeat after me:
Good morning, Doctor. You have a nice surgery. My problem is easy to describe. When I get work back from my teacher I see spots all over the page.

You've done that?
You're cured!

35

PATIENT –

Good afternoon, Doctor. My teacher says my sentences are really boring. They really are. They're just dull. They're also boring.

DOCTOR –

(Yawn) I see. You sound to me as if you do use full stops, which is encouraging. Did you realize that you can also use question marks to end sentences?

PATIENT –
Really?

DOCTOR –
Or you can use exclamation marks!

PATIENT –
That's amazing!

DOCTOR –

Just make sure that you don't overdose on them. Too many question marks and exclamation marks can be bad news. I would also suggest that you try to vary the length of your sentences. Use short ones when dramatic events are occurring.

PATIENT –

He staggered into the room. He held his stomach. Blood gushed out. He collapsed, dead.

DOCTOR –

Very good! And use long ones when you are being more reflective or descriptive.

PATIENT –

I like the way your surgery walls are painted in a blushing pink, with the skirting board in a fresh, white gloss.

DOCTOR –

You seem to be getting better already. For an even more interesting effect, mix your sentence length.

PATIENT –

Are you trying to suggest that intelligent, entertaining essays have a variety of sentence lengths? I see!

DOCTOR –

Thank you!
Next patient, please.

PATIENT –

Hello, Doctor. I've come to see you despite being scared of doctors because my mother my over-protective worrying mother is concerned that I never ever use commas not even occasionally.

DOCTOR –

This might be because you've never been sure of the procedures regarding the use of commas.

PATIENT –

My friend says you just use them for pauses in sentences.

DOCTOR –

Most definitely not.

Use commas when:

1. There's a list in your sentence and you want to separate the items in it...

I am a warm, witty, wonderful human being.

The field was waterlogged, the fans were soaking, the amp threatened to blow up, but the band carried on playing.

2. You're fitting in an extra point in your sentence. Use one comma if the point's at the beginning or end of a sentence...

I hate turkey, especially at Christmas.

With a huge yawn, I turned over and went back to sleep.

Or use two commas around the point if it's in the middle of the sentence...

The Goth, whose name was Neil, wore piercings and had dyed his hair black.

3. When you're introducing direct speech (that is quoting someone else's words using speech marks)...

> The bouncer said, "We don't want your sort here."
>
> **4.** When your sentence is addressed to someone, to separate off his or her name...
>
> I hate you, Tom.
>
> **5.** When you have a little question added on to your sentence...
>
> This purple lipstick's nice, isn't it?
>
> **6.** When you need a comma to help make the sense clearer...
>
> The bigger the car, the more petrol it consumes.

PATIENT –
  So I should have said, "Hello, Doctor. I've come to see you, despite being scared of doctors, because my mother, my over-protective, worrying mother, is concerned that I never, ever use commas, not even occasionally?

DOCTOR –
  I think you're cured.

Spice up your sentences!

Bored with using the same old punctuation marks day in, day out? Then choose from our exciting selection below to give your sentences that special something.

Brackets can be used instead of commas to section off an extra part of your sentence. Use them only if your sentence still makes sense without the bit in the brackets.

The Reeback trainers with battery-operated springs (on page 27 of our catalogue) are bound to improve your stamina!

Dashes can be used to add extra bits to sentences, for that dramatic flourish.

He came and sat down by me, put his arm over my shoulder, turned his face so it was directly in front of mine, took off his glasses – and proceeded to eat them!

Colons can be used to introduce lists, long quotations or speeches in playscripts. They mark a major break in a sentence.

There are four excellent reasons why I'll never go out with you: you're shorter than me, you're far too hairy, you smell, and your name is Rover.

 Semicolons can join two short, related sentences when you might be – wrongly – tempted to use a comma. Or use semicolons instead of a full stop when you have two sentences that link in some way.

The phone's ringing; I'll get it.

 Three dots (an ellipse) are great for letting a dramatic sentence trail away suggestively, because three dots mean something is being left out.

"Hello, Karen. I just thought…"
"Yes, Steve?"
"I wondered if you'd like…"
"Yes? Don't be shy!"
"If you'd like to know your jumper's on back to front."

Fit punctuation marks into the following sentences:

1. And tonight's lottery numbers are 12, 16, 32, 34 __
2. I love you __ will you marry me?
3. In WestEnders __ on at 8 o'clock tonight __ Bert is run over by a fork-lift truck.
4. No, your cat is not fat __ she's pregnant!

Answers on page 220.

Somebody else's sentences

There will be times in your writing when you'll want to use other people's sentences:

- if you're telling a story with *dialogue* (talking) in it
- if you're *quoting* from a text.

When you use other people's words you have to acknowledge that fact by using quotation marks ("...").

> "May I join you?" he asked.
> "Why? Am I coming apart?" Melanie replied.

Remember that, in dialogue, fresh speeches always start on fresh lines, slightly in from the margin – just like new paragraphs.

There is detailed help on quoting from books on page 172. For now, just remember that the punctuation mark that ends the sentence goes *before* the final quotation mark.

> **We know William is a sinister character because the writer describes him as "shifty, with eyes that seem to follow you around the room."**

Stop for a minute. My head's beginning to spin with all these different punctuation marks. There are so many rules I'll never learn them all.

You will. The more you practise them, the more they'll make sense to you. It's a bit like learning to drive – there are a lot of complicated things to remember, but once you're driving properly, you do the right things automatically. Just hang on in there! Concentrate on one rule every week – take one step at a time.

And the other thing that gets me is all this jargon you use. Colons and semicolons and apostrophes...

Ah ... yes ... apostrophes

In fact, apostrophes are dead easy. They sound complicated but an apostrophe (') is just a marker for missing letters. If you take a letter or letters away from a word, you put in an apostrophe to show what you've done.

"They are." Take away the "a", put in an apostrophe and you've got "they're".

Look at these examples:

Can't = can + not   we're = we + are
Mustn't = must + not   I'll = I + will
Nothin' = nothing   won't = wol + not

What was that? Wol not? I've never heard of that.

That's because "wol not" is Old English for "will not". The abbreviation "won't" actually means "will not". Stay with me and you'll see why I'm telling you this. Finding out about Old English will make apostrophes a whole lot easier.

Old English?
What's that?

I'll explain. The English language isn't a fixed thing. Ever since people first started speaking English, the language has been changing – changing its spellings, its grammar, its pronunciation, even its letters. Look at this:

Faeder ure,
Thu the eart on heofonum,
Si thin nama gehalgod.

That's Old English, or more precisely, Anglo-Saxon. It's actually the opening of the Lord's Prayer in Anglo-Saxon.

Weird.

Moving on to the fourteenth century, the language changes again. You might find it's a little more like modern English now. This is the opening of Geoffrey Chaucer's famous poem "The Canterbury Tales".

44

Whan that Aprill with his shoures soote
The droghte of March hath perced to the roote...

> Yeah, I can recognize some of the words there. The spelling's strange, though. He likes ending words with "e", doesn't he?

I was hoping you'd notice that. He writes "soote ... droghte ... roote" and we say "sweet ... drought ... root". There's a reason for that. In Old English there were letters at the ends of words to show what job the word had in the sentence. Word order wasn't so important. It was the letters at the end of the word which counted.

For example, if a man had a hawk, a scribe would write

The mannes hawk

The "es" showed the hawk belonged to the man.

During Chaucer's time, the Middle Ages, folk got lazy and stopped putting the ends on words. When Chaucer was writing, you can see this process happening – the ends of the words had only half-fallen off, leaving an "e". That's why you get odd "e"s tagged on to the ends of words. Now we no longer have extra letters on the ends of words – with one exception.

To show *belonging*.

We don't write *the mannes hawk*. We write *the man's hawk*, leaving out the "ne". That's why we write apostrophe + s ('s), to show belonging.

For example...

> **Rachel's job is to clean Dad's car...**
> **Matt's job is to empty the washer...**
> **James's job is to remind everyone else about their jobs...**

Note – even though James ends in "s", he still gets an 's to show something belongs to him. BUT plural words already have the extra "s" on the end (to show there is more than one), so you only add an apostrophe to show belonging.

> **The three witches' cauldron**
> **The boys' football team**
> **The bees' hive**

I get that. But I've got a query. I thought words like "yours" and "mine" showed belonging. Do they need an apostrophe?

No. Here's a list of words that show belonging but don't have an apostrophe:

mine	ours	yours
his	hers	its
their	whose	

As in, *that book is yours, the bag is hers.*

Most of all, notice that the word "its" – when it shows belonging – **doesn't** need an apostrophe…

> **The dog wagged its tail.**

It's always means *it is.*

> **It's cold outside.**
> **It's time for an equalizer.**

Now you've read this section, you'll never misuse an apostrophe again, although plenty of people do. Look out for billboards, posters, etc. where the apostrophe is put in the wrong place. Snigger, by all means, but please don't tell the poor shopkeeper who wrote "Lettuce's only 30p" that *lettuces* is a plural and therefore doesn't need an apostrophe at all, otherwise he might fling his choicest Iceberg at you!

Grrr ... rammar!

The rules of English grammar can be hard to grasp as a lot of them are based on Latin. Not only that, but the way we use English is changing all the time and this affects grammar as well.

We call the form of the verb that starts with "to" *the infinitive*, like, to sing, to eat, and to go. It used to be bad form to split the infinitive, as in "to loudly sing" – better to say "to sing loudly". Since Star Trek and its catchphrase "to boldly go where no man has gone before" some people accept that it's OK to split an infinitive. Or should I say, to boldly split an infinitive?

Here is one rule that still applies – make sure you follow it: don't change tenses in the middle of a sentence otherwise your reader won't know the time of day!

Look how confusing this example is:

> I am hungry. So I went into the kitchen and I am putting a pizza in the microwave. That will be a big mistake. It went all hard and rubbery but I will eat it anyway.

See how much easier it is to read when it's all in the same tense.

> I was hungry. So I went into the kitchen and put a pizza in the microwave. That was a big mistake. It went all hard and rubbery but I ate it anyway.

There are other grammar rules that might trip you up, but as with spelling, it's best to tackle these as they come up in your writing. Learning too many grammar rules at once can cause severe mental congestion. If your teacher tells you something in your writing doesn't sound right, nag him or her until you understand what it is you've done wrong. And remember: read, read, read! The more you read, the more you'll effortlessly absorb good grammar.

Handwriting

Even if your spelling, punctuation and grammar are flawless, you still might not get the grade you deserve if the examiner can't read what you've written. This is why clear handwriting is the most important skill there is. (Unless, of course, your spelling, punctuation and grammar are so bad you want to disguise it from the examiner…) P.S. Don't take that last suggestion seriously.

Handwriting must be readable in both coursework and exam work. Check you don't fall into any of the following categories:

The Miniaturist

The trouble I have with the opposite sex is that I can never work out....

The handwriting here is so minute that the examiner needs a microscope.

The Blockhead

EXACTLY WHAT IT IS they're trying to say

This candidate writes in a block, not making the tails and heads of letters long enough. Result? Illegibility – it's unreadable.

The Airhead

I'm free as a breeze man!

Here not all the letters are formed correctly, with many not joined up. The examiner keeps the script for a family game at Christmas time, called Guess What The Candidate Means.

The Roundhead

millions of kids think its wicked to write like this.

This candidate attempts to look trendy by dotting "i"s with circles. It's time-wasting, and might irritate the kind of examiner who's been brought up to believe that because the rest of the world dots "i"s with dots, you should too.

The Terminally Indecisive

I'm the ~~soft~~ sort ∧ of ~~person~~ girl person who ~~spends~~ ages A in ~~in the changing rooms~~ all her time in shops ~~deciding~~ choosing ~~especially~~ I like ~~Firer Island and~~ New Look for shopping.

The examiner needs a route map to find his or her way through this. It takes three times as long to read as everybody else's script and the Cup Final's about to begin in five minutes. Do you fancy this candidate's chances? No way.

So how's your handwriting? If people have ever complained they can't read what you've written, you've got a problem. Don't worry if you're just untidy. Being a little untidy is OK, and under exam conditions nearly everyone is untidy.

If you're a crosser-outer, your mind is probably racing ahead of your pen. Try slowing down, and plan carefully what you want to say so that you don't keep changing your mind. Or you might just be incredibly nervous. So take a few deep breaths, smile at nothing in particular, and try to relax!

What needs desperate action is handwriting that can't be deciphered...

Action plan

1. Get someone to analyse your handwriting. What is your problem? Are you not joining letters up? Making too many loops? Decide what you need to improve on.

2. Make a list of the improvements you need to make, including any letters that you need to form differently.

3. Each week, introduce one change to your handwriting. For example, if you form "y"s incorrectly, spend a week just concentrating on the letter "y" and nothing else. It will take you this long to make a permanent change.

4. In following weeks, make more changes.

5. Sit back, and let the compliments roll in!

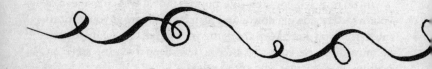

Hands up who hates comprehension?

In your GCSE exam you're bound to come across a passage to read with questions attached. This section will help you to tackle them.

> Good. Because I can't stand comprehensions. I'll tell you the worst thing about them. They're sooo boring.

Granted. Whenever you have to go over something several times, it can get boring. But if you know exactly what you're looking for and there's an end in sight, it's not too bad.

> I still prefer renting a good video.

Well, that's your *opinion*. Your teacher's *opinion* might be that it's worth knowing how to do a comprehension properly. The *fact* is, if you're taking English GCSE, you will need to do a comprehension-type study.

What's with all this fact and opinion business?

Examiners are keen that you can tell the difference between fact and opinion. That's one of the basic skills they want you to have.

FACT = something no one can disagree with, something that can be proved, e.g.

> **You are reading this book.**
> **Africa is a large continent.**
> **Sophie is 5'6" with brown, curly hair.**

OPINION = the feeling of one person or a group of people about a fact, your view, the way you see things, e.g.

> **This is a good book.**
> **Africa isn't worth going to because of the mosquitoes.**
> **Sophie is a babe.**

Who says Sophie is a babe? Personally, I prefer blondes. And she always looks in a mood. And…
   If there's room for disagreement, you're looking at an opinion.
   Keeping in mind the difference between fact and opinion will help you navigate your way through the passage-based questions.

When you say a "passage", what exactly do you mean? Do the examiners make things up to test us on?

No. They choose passages. These could come from a newspaper, magazine, biography, autobiography, pamphlet, advertisement, newsletter, travel guide, manual, encyclopaedia entry – the list is endless. The examination boards generally let you know in advance whether it's fiction or non-fiction that will be on your paper. A fiction passage is what is called *literary* – taken from a novel or short story – and non-fiction is *non-literary* – basically anything else. Most comprehensions these days are non-literary, and a tip is that the majority of them seem to be taken from newspapers.

Right! So I should start reading *The Sun*, then.

Not *The Sun*, I'm afraid. Try the broadsheet newspapers such as *The Times*, *Guardian*, *Telegraph* and *Independent*. Reading one of these from time to time is an excellent preparation for GCSE English. If you find these newspapers heavy-going, begin by reading articles that interest you – maybe sport or music, celebrity interviews, animal rights, etc., and just get the feel of the way they use language.

Afraid not. The more you read, the more you'll begin to understand. Answering exam questions on passages is all about showing the examiner you've understood what you've read.

I suppose you think you're funny.

Right, let's get down to business. First we'll have a look at the different types of passage that might come up in your exam, and then all the skills and techniques you'll need to answer questions on them. Then we'll apply those skills to a real passage and see how far they take us.

Passages

Before we start, it's important to remember that all forms of writing have a PURPOSE.

> **A shopping list**
> – to remind you to get the right things at the shops
>
> **The note you passed in Biology**
> – to distract your mate with terrible jokes
>
> **The election leaflet**
> – to get you to vote for that party
>
> **The instructions on the video recorder**
> – to let you know how it works
>
> **A short story**
> – to entertain you or to make you think
>
> **This book**
> – to get you a brilliant grade at GCSE

Whenever you read anything, get into the habit of working out what its purpose is. *Why* has it been written? *Who* has it been written *for*?

When you've worked that out, you can move on to thinking about *how* the passage works – what methods does the writer use to do the job? Every trade requires tools – car mechanics have spanners, hairdressers have blow dryers, and writers have tools too.

Only they're harder to spot... Or are they?

> informal address
>
> flattery
>
> *Hi Kevin!*
>
> *My mate Jane thinks you're dead cute. You don't know Jane but her dad's the Chairman of Westchester Rovers. She usually hangs out around the bike sheds at lunchtime. See ya!*
>
> *Maggie.*
>
> friendly tone   so you know where to find her   bribery

Not great literature, but pretty effective. And not a bad analysis either. Now for the real McCoy. Take a look at this.

Factual writing

The most basic sort of non-literary material is writing which is only designed to give you information.

> **Screen One.** *The Return of the Killer Gnats II.*
> 12.30 pm, 4.15 pm, 8.00 pm.

Other examples of informative writing might be your school textbooks, the Highway Code, operating instructions or an encyclopaedia.

HOW TO WALK

1. Stand with both feet planted firmly on the ground.
2. Push against the floor with the toes of your right foot, raise your right knee until the whole of your foot is lifted off the ground.
3. Straighten your right leg and place your right foot approximately six inches ahead of your left foot.

WARNING: Do not place right foot directly in front of left foot or you will get tangled.

4. The momentum caused by step 3 will propel left leg forward.
5. Push down on ground with left foot and repeat movement three on left side.
6. Continue sequence as rapidly as is necessary for effective ambulation. Note: the further forward you place your foot, the greater the stride.

This is a set of instructions, and as such is perfectly clear. The writer only has one intention, which is to convey information.

The methods used include:

- A numbered list
- Giving the information in the form of orders
  (stand, raise, push down)
- Precise words (straighten, propel)
- Technical words (momentum, ambulation)

Most straightforward informative writing uses methods like these. Also graphs, statistics and tables might be given as pure information.

Expressing opinion

Very often a writer doesn't only want to give information, but also an *opinion* on the information. A lot of the articles you read in magazines and newspapers are like this. Some are quite obviously relaying opinions, for example, letters on the letter page, or a column about why stick-thin supermodels set a bad example to teenage girls.

In other articles the opinions might not be so obvious. You might be reading a moving piece about the plight of the homeless, and you think you're being moved by the *facts*, but you are also being affected by the way the writer is expressing himself. He might be stating an *indirect opinion* by using dramatic words, or choosing to single out a particular homeless person and making us identify with his or her predicament.

As a GCSE student, you've got to be on the lookout for indirect opinion.

Here are two examples of writers expressing opinions. In the first it's quite easy to see the opinions being expressed:

Nothing makes me see red more than a holier-than-thou vegetarian. Priggishly they refuse to eat meat for "moral reasons", therefore suggesting we meat eaters are fundamentally immoral. "Meat is murder" they cry in their whining, insistent voices. Meat isn't murder. Mother Nature intended us to eat meat. Our digestive systems are geared to processing meat. Man's earliest occupation was that of hunter, and we didn't go out with our bows and arrows to hunt lettuce leaves! Murder is one human being killing another; consuming other animals is something many species do in order to survive. And what about all the butchers who would be out of work if vegetarians had their way? Is it moral to cause mass unemployment for butchers?

This writer is presenting a one-sided argument, and it's easy to spot the opinions:

✔ Hates "moral" vegetarians.
✔ Dislikes the way they claim they are "better" than meat-eaters.
✔ Thinks they criticize everyone else.
✔ Thinks it's natural to eat meat.
✔ Thinks it's essential for our survival to eat meat.

There *are* some facts lurking in there, such as hunting being man's earliest occupation, but the writer doesn't use the facts to make a convincing case for meat-eating now.

In conveying these opinions, this writer uses certain *techniques* or tools. Here are just four of them.

- ✔ The writer builds a stereotypical picture of a vegetarian as priggish (self-righteous), whining and narrow-minded.
- ✔ The short sentences with their pounding rhythms sound like the writer's making a speech.
- ✔ The writer uses the word "we" implicitly including you, the reader, whether you like it or not!
- ✔ The writer asks questions to draw in the reader. Notice that the last question is one that doesn't really expect an answer – this is called a *rhetorical question*.

Can you see the difference between the opinions, and the tricks used to express them?

Now read the next passage, where the opinion is stated more subtly.

A recent survey supported claims that 60% of teenagers watch more than two hours of television a day. This alarming statistic suggests one reason for the increasing materialism among young adults: constant exposure to advertisements will stimulate demand for consumer goods. Sales of fashionable trainers (manufactured at slave wages in developing countries) and designer clothes have reached an all-time high. A teenager exposed to a deluge of advertisements will be brainwashed into believing that acquiring the right status symbols confers social success. It is a sad fact that this is almost true; having the wrong trainers, or the wrong jeans, can spell social disaster for the unlucky victim. As teenagers begin to free themselves from the rule of their parents, they become subject to a new tyranny – that of the manufacturers of fashion items.

This writer has as strong an opinion as the first writer – that teenagers spend far too much money on designer wear. Nowhere is this opinion actually stated. Instead it's implied in everything the writer says. The opinion is conveyed in the language – in the tricks the writer uses. Here are some of them:

✔ The use of statistics suggests the writer is being scientifically accurate and has proof for his opinions.

✔ The writer describes these statistics as "alarming" which suggests it's very bad that teenagers watch so much television.

✔ Using more complex, technical language ("stimulate demand for consumer goods") makes the writer sound as if he or she has authority, and knows what he or she is talking about.

✔ The phrase "slave wages" is very emotive, i.e. it plays on your emotions, and is used to get in a dig at how people in developing countries are exploited by fashion companies.

✔ The use of the words "deluge" and "brainwash" suggests teenagers are being robbed of their free will.

✔ "Tyranny" compares fashion manufacturers to dictatorial rulers – strong stuff!

Looking at *how* writers express themselves can often reveal their opinions.

Yeah.
I can see that.
It's like my mum. If she says
"Can you tidy your room later?"
I know she's not that bothered, so I
don't do it. But if she says "Tidy your
room NOW or you're grounded!" I
go and hide a few things under
the bed...

Well done! You got it absolutely. It's HOW you express yourself that counts in English GCSE, and in life.

Cool!
But is there a list of
techniques you could
give me that writers use, so
I could look for them
in passages?

Unfortunately, no. There are as many techniques as there are writers. But do watch out for the following favourites:

- emotive language
- exaggeration
- similes and metaphors
- using the word "we"
- repetition
- rhetorical questions
- careful choice of words (the English language jargon for "choice of words" is *diction*).

A simile is a comparison using "like" or "as" – "he felt as wobbly as jelly" or "the engine purred like a cat".
A metaphor is a comparison which doesn't use "like" or "as" – "I was shattered after the gig".

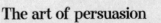

The art of persuasion

So far we've looked at purely factual writing, and writing that expresses an opinion. A third sort of writing is persuasive writing – where the intention of the writer is to force you to believe what he or she is saying. You're most likely to meet persuasive writing in advertisements, and advertisements do have a habit of cropping up on GCSE papers.

Take a look at the one over the page.

COPOFF – THE MAGIC INGREDIENT WITH THE ULTIMATE PULLING POWER.

COPOFF

SPECIAL OFFER! SPECIAL OFFER!

You know the feeling. You're down at the club, and the person you fancy is standing by the bar. Your stomach does a back flip. Shyly you glance in his or her direction. He – or she – gives you the once-over, then looks away, uninterested.

You try sidling up to the object of your desires; you might even venture a 'hello' or employ your favourite chat-up line. No reaction. Suddenly an evening in with your Physics revision seems an attractive proposition. What is it with you? Why does nobody ever fancy you?

Sadly you make your way home, wondering whether you need GCSEs for entering a monastery.

BUT HELP IS AT HAND!!!

Did you know that sexual attraction is not primarily a matter of appearance? Have you noticed that it isn't always the best-looking babes that get the blokes? Or the drop-dead gorgeous guys who get the gals?

Scientists in the USA have been working secretly for years on the new compound Pherocopamine-A, the essential ingredient of sexual attraction. This pro-hormone with its added ingredient of selenio-zirconium has been proven in the laboratory to make the saddest individual into a sex-God – or Goddess.

Most Hollywood superstars and chart-topping boy bands have been using it for years.

Now scientists have developed a way to mass-produce Pherocopamine-A, and it can be safely added to your own favourite scent.

YOU CAN COUNT ON COPOFF!!

In tests, 999 out of 1,000 people said their love lives had improved dramatically after adding COPOFF to their perfume or aftershave. The one person who gave a negative response was on the way to the post office to collect his pension.

Only
£12.99
from all reputable chemists!

SPECIAL OFFER! SPECIAL OFFER!
Buy COPOFF in bulk and collect your free FILE-A-DATE personal organizer – essential for keeping your crazy love life under control.

If you're asked questions about an advertisement like this, chances are the examiner will want you to single out the writer's techniques and find examples of their use. Since you're not in an English exam yet, but only reading this book, we're going to help you.

The following are just some of the techniques in this advertisement – *you* find quotes from the ad that show the technique in use.

1. Pseudo-scientific jargon to convince you the product works.

2. Statistics to show it works.

3. Celebrity endorsement (if they use it, it must be good).

4. Slang that targets a teen consumer.

5. Slogans

6. Humour

How did you get on? Look on page 220 and see if you came up with some good examples.

A method for tackling comprehensions

Now you've looked at four passages, you're almost ready to move on to the hard stuff – the questions themselves. But first, you'll need a method for answering comprehension questions...

1. Reading the passage

Faced with a passage in the exam, the first thing you've got to do is read it. That's stating the obvious. But did you know that *how* you read can make a big difference to the way you answer the questions?

In an exam, you're bound to be nervous and that will affect your reading skills. You'll be all tensed up, easily distracted, and worried that you're not understanding what you're reading. The first thing to do, then, is to relax. Remember that the examiner wouldn't give you this passage if he or she didn't think you'd be able to get the gist of it. Have faith in yourself!

Try this method of reading the passage:

- Pick up a pencil.

- Read the first paragraph, underlining what seem to you to be the important bits.

- When you've read the first paragraph, jot down by the side of it what you think that paragraph is trying to say – the point it's trying to make.

- Do the same for the next paragraphs until you've finished.

- At the end, think about the whole passage and what it is about. Look at your notes to help you.

If you like, you can put down this book now, find a newspaper or magazine, and practise reading an article in this way. It makes you feel very studious and focussed – give it a go!

This reading-with-a-pencil method is for your initial read of the passage. You *will* be reading the passage again later, but in a different way.

2. Reading the Questions

Once you've got an idea of the passage, it's time to look at the questions. The most common way to *lose* marks at GCSE is by not reading and answering the questions properly.

OK. Now get a piece of paper, read through these instructions and follow them carefully.

---

1. Write out your name.

2. Write the figure 3 in the top left-hand corner of your piece of paper.

3. Underline your name three times – you do not need to use a ruler.

4. Write out your date of birth immediately below it.

5. Place a finger on your forehead.

6. Do none of the above.

Did you fall for that? If you'd read to the end before starting the instructions, you'd have saved yourself a lot of work.

> **TOP TIP**
> It is just as important to read the questions properly as it is to read the passage properly.

Again, take your pencil and underline the important words or phrases or instructions in the questions. Get in your head exactly what it is you're being asked to do. Try not to do anything else. Getting the question firmly fixed in your head is probably the most important part of the whole exercise.

> **TOP TIP**
> Sometimes the examiners actually try and help you. Often the first question is directed at one part of the passage, and the second (or third) at others. So if you find you keep going back to the same part of the passage for your evidence, you might have gone wrong. It's worth checking!

And remember – everything you write from now on must be *in answer to the question*. Never be tempted just to write out what's in the passage hoping it will do. It won't. Think how silly it would be in real life if people did that.

Dad – can I have a CD player for my room?

Do you know how much a CD player costs? Do you know how much I had to shell out on the car last week? You waste enough time in your room listening to your radio as it is. When I was your age I didn't even know what a CD player was – they hadn't even been invented. I had to save up to have one play on the juke box...

Infuriating, isn't it?

So *always* answer the question exactly as it is set.

Another good tip with questions is to rephrase them in your own mind, in words that are more familiar to you, so the question seems more answerable. For example, this is a real question taken from an English GCSE paper:

> **Compare article 1 with article 2.**
> **You should write about:**
> ● **what the writers are setting out to do**
> ● **how they present information**
> ● **how they use language**
> ● **how successful they are.**

In your mind, you translate like this:

> I've got to write about both passages...
> 1 The aims of the writers, why they've written those passages, see if there are different reasons...
> 2 The order they tell us stuff in, any tricks they use to make their information clear, their methods.
> 3 The words they use or their phrases, especially good ones.
> 4 Which one I prefer <u>and why</u> – don't forget the good points of the other passage too.

Just translate the question using your own words, and the translation will act as a guide for you, so you stay on the right tracks.

3. Research

It sounds crazy, but the worst thing you can do in passage-based questions is to start writing immediately. I know you're aware that time is passing and you must get a move on, but just writing without planning is a recipe for disaster. The examiners build in time for you to think – they HATE long, waffly, rambling answers that don't answer the questions. They prefer answers that are shorter and to the point.

75

Use part of the time you're given in the exam to think through what you are going to say and to research your answers. This is where you read the passage or passages through for a *second* time, this time bearing those all-important questions firmly in mind. As you read the passage again, look for material that might help you answer the questions or perform the tasks the examiner has set.

At this stage you are a sort of private detective searching for clues. Hidden in that there passage is the stuff that will get you a good grade. Your task is to find it. Spend your time doing this, and you won't go far wrong. Underline or put squiggles by the stuff you find, storing it for later. It doesn't matter if your question paper is a mess, as long as you understand the significance of your underlinings and squiggles.

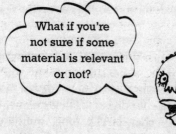

Include it anyway!

TOP TIP
In English exams, if you write down something that is wrong, you don't get marks knocked off. You get zero marks. So the best policy if you're not sure whether a point is right or not is to include it briefly. This is not the same as waffling – it's taking a calculated risk!

So there you are, marking the passage and sorting out all the info that's going to help you start answering the questions in a minute. Only start writing when you've got something solid to write about. Marshal your facts, get your ammunition together – know where you're going. Remember: **think** and **plan** before you write.

4. Writing your answer
Here are two guaranteed-to-work tips to make your writing effective:

a) Keep reminding the examiner you're really answering the question by referring to the original wording of the question. E.g. if the question says "what methods does the writer use" *you say* "one of the methods the writer uses is…"

b) As far as possible, use your own words. Very often it reminds you in the question to use your own words. This is important because if you just copy from the passage, how does the examiner know if you've understood it? Copying isn't the same as understanding. So one of the main skills in answering passage-based questions is being able to put things in your own words. You don't have to have a hugely impressive vocabulary to do this, just use ordinary, everyday words (not slang – more about this in the section on writing on page 149).

Most of the time you don't have to be brilliantly clever to do well in comprehension, but just have the knack of making relevant points and putting them in your own words.

5. Prove it

Whenever you make a point or state an opinion in your answer, prove it by finding something from the passage to back up your point. This may be a *brief* quotation, or just a fact or two. If you can prove what you are saying you will get double the credit for it. Remember all those underlinings and squiggles you made earlier? They will help you find the evidence to back up your answer. Just as in a court of law, evidence is vital.

Time, now, to put these skills to the test.

The following article by reporter Sam Hart is taken from *The Big Issue*. Read it through carefully.

> Picture the scene – it's a sunny afternoon and you are enjoying a quiet drink in a pavement café. Suddenly there is a deafening explosion, a column of flame leaps into the air and a huge lump of concrete is hurtling towards your head. Is it a vicious terrorist attack? No, it's an exploding manhole cover.
>
> This may sound suspiciously like a scene from *Mission Impossible*, but it's a very real – and potentially lethal – phenomenon.
>
> Last August, Mark Woodward, a 33-year-old film-maker, was sitting outside a busy café in London's Covent Garden. "From nowhere there was this massive explosion, followed by an incredibly loud and sinister buzzing sound," he recalls. "Everyone dived to the floor and then a flame shot eight feet into the air. There was total shock and panic, children were crying, tables were overturned and there was an awful smell of burning chemicals. We assumed that the IRA had put a bomb in a bin."

In fact, the traumatized customers were casualties of an exploding manhole. Woodward had to undergo a hernia operation as a direct result of injuries he sustained, and three people, including a pregnant woman, were hospitalized. Student and waitress, Raffaella Galasso, was one of them. She sustained first and second degree burns to both her legs. She says: "The pain was terrible, I couldn't move my legs at all."

The scars from the horrific burns will be with Galasso for the rest of her life – and she claims: "I was absolutely terrified. It changed my life completely. I became an incredibly nervous person. Even the tiniest little thing like someone turning a tap on suddenly would make me jump. I couldn't use the Underground for ages and even now taking a tube or getting a lift makes me nervous. I am terrified of being caught in another explosion."

Faulty wiring in cable boxes underneath manhole covers is one cause of these explosions and several people are still seeking compensation from the London Electricity Board for last year's incident. Defective cables smoulder and burn their insulating plastic, causing a build-up of gas. When the insulation has melted, the wiring can spark and ignite the accumulated gases. The resulting fire can cause an explosion forceful enough to blow the manhole cover several feet into the air.

A spokesperson for the LEB says such cases are extremely rare, but the *Big Issue* has learned of at least three incidents of erupting covers during the past year in London alone, including an occasion when a Norwegian tourist was injured when the pavement literally exploded beneath his feet.

Neither the fire brigade nor the electricity board collect figures on these alarming episodes, but the journal of strange phenomena, *Fortean Times*, has been conducting its own research and has unearthed a series of exploding manhole covers worldwide. And, it seems, faulty cable boxes aren't always to blame. Build-up of air pressure, excess rain and methane gas are among the possible explanations for the occurrences.

Joe McNally, associate editor of the magazine says: "It's a very odd story. When you look at the various incidents, you see that there are a wide variety of explanations, but they aren't always satisfactory. For example, we have a case of a car damaged very severely by a manhole cover landing on top of it. The official explanation for the explosion was air pressure, but that didn't go any way to explaining the violence of the blast."

The thought that potential death traps lurk beneath our pavements is not a comforting one. And survivors like Mark Woodward believe more should be done to safeguard the public. "I am incredibly angry about the whole thing. I was lucky but who knows what could happen to someone next time? These covers were obviously designed without public safety in mind. There must be some way of installing a safety device to deflect the blast."

Raffaella Galasso agrees. "It was the most terrible experience of my life, but I have received no apology from anyone. It was a lovely sunny day, and all of a sudden this nightmare happened and changed my life for ever."

Done that? I promise you, it IS safe to walk the streets. You're more likely to be hit by a bus than an exploding manhole cover.

Back to comprehension skills. You should have taken in that the article was about the dangers posed by exploding manhole covers and what causes this phenomenon. You will also have noticed that a large part of the article is the reported speech of people who were injured by an exploding manhole cover. For a first read-through, that's good enough. In fact, you're now ready for the questions…

1. **What different reasons are given in this passage to explain why manhole covers explode? (5)**
2. **How does the writer convey the frightening nature of the threat posed by exploding manhole covers? (10)**

It's important to look very carefully at these questions and suss them out properly.

The first thing to notice is the marks allotted to them. Those marks in brackets are probably the most helpful part of the exam paper because it's the examiner telling you *how much he wants you to write*. If question 1 is worth 5 marks and question 2 is worth 10 marks, then you've got to write twice as much for question 2.

Every English exam you take, from whatever board, will have the marks printed on them in this way. Always use them as a timing guide – there's more about timing in the final chapter of this book starting on page 202.

Let's take the first question first. We have to find the reasons why manhole covers explode. That seems straightforward enough. Examiners call these kind of questions "search-and-find". The info's in the passage, and like the little bloodhound you are, you've just got to go fetch.

Having read the passage once, you're already familiar with it, and you might have formed the impression that the reasons why manhole covers explode are tucked away in the middle. However, you want to be careful, so you begin by skim-reading the whole passage to check you haven't missed anything.

First paragraph … description of an exploding manhole cover … hmm. No reasons given there … then the story of Mark Woodward … no reasons given there … then Raffaella Galasso's experiences and injuries … no reasons there … hmm … hmm… Aha!! It says "Faulty wiring in cable boxes underneath manhole covers is one cause of these explosions".

So you underline that and read on. In the rest of that paragraph there's more technical information … "Defective cables smoulder and burn their insulating plastic, causing a build-up of gas. When the insulation has melted, the wiring can spark and ignite the accumulated gases. The resulting fire can cause an explosion…"

You underline that and look at it again. Is this another reason why manhole covers explode? In fact, it isn't. It's only a more detailed explanation of how faulty wiring in cable boxes can lead to explosions. You pause and bite your lip. Do you include that?

You read on. Aha again! In the next paragraph but one, it says "faulty cable boxes aren't always to blame. Build-up of air pressure, excess rain and methane gas are among the possible explanations…" You underline that. It's going to be useful.

You carry on reading. Joe McNally says those explanations aren't satisfactory, but he doesn't say what other explanations there are. Your question asks you to focus only on the reasons. You don't underline anything. McNally also mentions air pressure, but you've already got that one.

You read to the end, in case you've missed something. But there are only comments on the danger and quotes from Woodward and Galasso. The end.

You look back over what you've underlined, and you should have this:

<u>Faulty wiring in cable boxes underneath manhole covers is one cause of these explosions…</u>

<u>Defective cables smoulder and burn their insulating plastic, causing a build-up of gas. When the insulation has melted, the wiring can spark and ignite the accumulated gases. The resulting fire can cause an explosion…</u>

<u>…faulty cable boxes aren't always to blame. Build up of air pressure, excess rain and methane gas are among the possible explanations for the occurrences…</u>

You look at the question again.

1. What different reasons are given in this passage to explain why manhole covers explode? (5)

83

You're reasonably happy. You can see you have four reasons (faulty wiring in cable boxes, build-up of air pressure, excess rain and methane gas) but the first reason comes with a longer explanation which would probably bring your mark total up to five if you include it.

You remember the relevant tips for writing up comprehension answers:
– Refer to the original wording of the question.
– Use your own words as far as possible.
So you begin:

> **The first reason given in the passage to explain why manhole covers explode is that the cable boxes have faulty wiring. Cables with faulty wiring will burn up the plastic surrounding them and that causes a build-up of gas. When all the plastic has melted the wire can spark and set alight all the gases. Other causes of exploding manhole covers include a build-up of air pressure, lots of rain and the presence of methane gas.**

And the examiner reads what you've written and awards you full marks. Yesss!

Notice how clever you've been here. You've used your own words when you can – like, "setting alight", instead of "ignite" – but where there's no substitute, e.g. "methane gas", you've left it alone. Part of the art of comprehension is knowing when you can put things in your own words, and when you can't. As with most things, practice makes perfect.

Now for question 2.

> **2. How does the writer convey the frightening nature of the threat posed by exploding manhole covers?**

Hold on!
I told you I found this
boring! So far I've had to
read that blasted passage three
times, and now I'm going to
have to do the same thing
again. Get a life!

Research is tedious, and I'd be a liar if I claimed otherwise. Search-and-tell questions are the most tedious of all, but they're good for scoring marks with, and at the end of the day you want a decent GCSE grade.

Anyway, the second question is loads more interesting because it isn't just about *what* the writer says, but *how* she says it. It's slightly more juicy.

Well, go
on, then...

In your own words, you're being asked what methods or tricks the writer uses to make the manhole cover explosions seem frightening.

At first glance, this looks difficult. When you first read a newspaper article you don't tend to look at how it's written, just as when you put on a CD, you listen to the music and don't spend ages peering at the CD player wondering how the laser makes the sounds! So don't worry if this question seems a little more challenging. You've just got to get yourself adjusted to a new perspective.

Time to re-read and research, looking for any ways at all in which the writer tries to scare us. Read through each of the 11 paragraphs and try to find as many points as possible. You can make your own list, then check out the list on page 221 to see how closely yours corresponds.

Take your time, there's a lot of information there. That's why it's so important to research carefully.

> You mean I was supposed to get all of that stuff at the back of the book?! My list was only a quarter as long as yours. I think I'll give up now...

Please don't. The good news is that examiners don't just mark you on how many points you get (though the more, the better) but also on how you explain yourself. A good explanation might earn you double the marks even if you have fewer points. They want to know how you *think*, and to judge that, they look at how you *express yourself*.

> Like ... er... doh!

You're fooling around again.

Having done your research, you can write up your answers. Just remember to:

- answer the question exactly
- use your own words as far as possible
- give evidence for your answer (quote from or refer to the passage).

Below are the beginnings of five answers to question two – only one of them is on the right lines. Can you decide which one is best?

a) It's a sunny afternoon and you are enjoying a quiet drink in a pavement café. Suddenly there is a deafening explosion, a column of flame leaps into the air and a huge lump of concrete is hurtling towards your head...

b) The writer makes the exploding manhole covers sound frightening by scaring you. You wouldn't want to have a manhole cover flying out at you, would you? She says it hurt two people and they had to go to hospital. That is frightening. It isn't nice to think that you could be walking along the street just minding your own business and a manhole cover jumps out at you. Not that the streets are very safe anyway. My gran tripped over a loose paving stone and had to go to casualty to get some stitches.

c) The writer frightens us by using language and describing a typical incident. You get the idea it could happen any time. A man called Mark Woodward was just sitting having a drink in a pavement café and he was injured by a flying manhole cover. He had to have an operation.

87

d) The writer uses several different methods to frighten the reader. In the first paragraph she asks us to imagine ourselves having a quiet drink outside, and then shocks us with the contrast of the chaos caused by an exploding manhole cover. She uses the second person "you" to address us directly. The words she uses to describe the exploding manhole cover incident are very dramatic, such as "deafening" ... "hurtling" ... "vicious".

e) The first method is describing an attack. She describes it well. The second method is describing what happens to people. She describes that well. The third method is describing what happens to you when you're attacked by a manhole cover. She describes that well. The fourth method...

The best answer? Definitely **d)**.

a) just copied out the passage. For this you'll get no marks at all. All it shows the examiner is that you were present in the examination room.

b) is a wonderful waffler. Rather than answering the question set she makes a few stray comments, then rabbits on about what she thinks about exploding manhole covers and her gran's injuries. She sounds a nice person, but I don't fancy her chances at GCSE.

c) begins by answering the question, although rather vaguely. What does he mean by saying the writer uses language? Surely all writers use language? They don't use clay or water colours. Then after answering the question very briefly, he goes on to give an account of the passage. Just repeating in your own words what is in the passage doesn't answer the question, and you won't get a lot of marks for it.

d) is the best one. See how he makes the points outlined in the research notes, and adds brief quotations to back up his points? It's clear he's answering the question. The examiner awards marks for each and every point, and sits back in his chair, smiling...

e) is mind-numbingly boring and says nothing. Indiscriminately praising writers isn't the same as analysing their methods. Good answers should always pick up on detail. This one doesn't. It also repeats words, which you should never do if you can avoid it. (Look out for our style tips on page 148.)

OK, OK. I get it.
But I'll never be able to write as well as d). I just can't stand reading model answers. They make me feel bad about what I can do...

I sympathize. But nobody expects you to write model answers – not your teachers, not your parents, not even the examiner.

If everyone gave model answers, I'd be out of a job!

All you have to do is improve on what you're doing now – you can only walk one step, or write one word, at a time.

But I still have problems.

OK. Tell me what they are…

What if…

…I run out of time?

Whenever you do a comprehension, whether in an exam, in class or at home, get into the habit of watching the clock. Before you start, do a few quick calculations to work out exactly how long you should spend on each sub-question, and make yourself stick to those time limits. (Check out page 215 for more detailed help on timing.) If you do run out of time and there are still points you want to make, jot them down in legible note form and then the examiner will give you some credit for them.

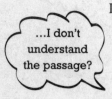

…I don't understand the passage?

It's highly unlikely you won't understand any of it. There may be parts that go over your head, but don't let that worry you too much. If you answer the questions relevantly using the parts of the passage you do understand, you'll be surprised at how well you can do.

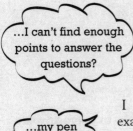

...I have to answer questions on two passages at once?

This might very well happen. You often get two passages on the same subject, but different in style. You might be asked to *compare and contrast* them, which means looking at the ways in which they are both similar and different. As a rule of thumb, point out similarities first, then differences. If you have to write at length about two passages, it's generally better to write about passage A first, then passage B, rather than dart about between them, otherwise you'll confuse the examiner and yourself. Most of the time in comprehensions, examiners will give you a series of bullet points to guide you through the comparison.

...I can't find enough points to answer the questions?

Don't spend too long looking for points that may not be there. Simply go into a lot of detail about the points you *can* find. That can earn you bonus marks if you explain yourself well.

...my pen runs out?

I wouldn't advise your leaving the examination hall to run after it.

Lucky tips!

- Practising passages with questions helps develop your skills, but if you haven't much time to practise, still get hold of as many old exam papers as you can and look carefully at how the questions are worded, i.e. practise *reading* questions. Old exam papers are available either from your English teacher or your exam board – the board might charge a small amount of money, but, come on, what are parents for?

Thanks Dad!

- Other sections of this book will also help to improve your comprehension. Look particularly at the essay writing section (on writing style) and exam technique sections.

- Get into the habit of always seeing passages as the work of a *writer*, not just words that appear magically on the page. The examiner is interested in reading what you have to say about what the writer does.

- If your mind goes blank with exam nerves, just remember these three brief golden rules, and you won't go far wrong:

  1. READ THE QUESTIONS CAREFULLY
  2. ANSWER THE QUESTIONS EXACTLY
  3. GIVE PROOF TO SUPPORT WHAT YOU SAY

Literary comprehensions

Some boards set passages that come from novels or short stories, some specially adapted to turn them into comprehensions. The way you tackle these is exactly the same as the way you would tackle non-literary comprehensions. Here's an example.

There was something Molly was wanting to ask Theresa.

She had nearly mentioned it as they were queueing at the black pudding stall in the market, each in their winter coats, buttoned right up to the top, each with their felt winter hats on, Molly's in pale green and Theresa's in maroon, but the girl in the white overall had sliced through the pudding in an instant and Molly had been distracted by the marbled pattern of the sausage and the girl's long, scarlet-painted fingernails. Theresa's lips were pursed distrustfully, and her eyes were locked on to the scales.

Later, Molly and Theresa had been sitting on the bus on their way back home, their shopping trolley with its square, black sides upright in the luggage compartment, frozen rigid with Theresa's steely gaze. Molly wondered if now might be the time, but as she prepared herself to speak Theresa pointed out of the bus window at a disused cinema that had now become a children's activity centre. She reminded Molly that in their day, before the war, the back alleys were good enough for playing in. Molly nodded in agreement.

Now if she didn't say anything, she knew she never would. Molly knew she was timid – Theresa had told her often enough, and so had Charles – and her small amount of resolve was trickling through her fingers like fine sand. She watched her older sister, hands sheathed in oven gloves, lift the casserole onto the asbestos mat on the kitchen table. Now, before she takes the lid off...

"I've been thinking of contacting Charles," said Molly.

"Contacting Charles!" Theresa was utterly incredulous. "But he's been dead for seven years!"

"Oh, I know you'll think I'm silly –" Molly laughed girlishly to concede this point, "but Mrs Plumstead – Hettie's neighbour – she's a medium, you know, and they say she's very good. And she doesn't charge a lot – she does it because it's a gift, you see, and I didn't think it would do any harm..."

Molly watched her sister's face. She was quite impassive. Then she lowered her eyelids fractionally and formed her lips into a shape resembling a smile, but a smile so satirical that even the casserole dish seemed to quail in submission.

"I'll be interested to see how you get on," she said.

Molly was astonished. Did this mean she had permission?

"Can I?" she asked, knowing that it was foolish for a woman of seventy-two to seek approval from her older sister for her actions, but unable to help herself. Molly had always been a good girl.

Theresa sniffed.

"You can do what you like. I'm surprised at you, Molly, believing all that twaddle."

1. What do you learn about the characters of the two sisters, and their relationship? (10 marks)

Here's the same passage again, but this time scrawled over by a candidate who's preparing to answer the question. Did you come up with any of these points?

94

There was something Molly was wanting to ask Theresa.

sounds like she's scared of mentioning it

She had nearly <u>mentioned</u> it as they

what's a black pudding?

were queueing at the black pudding stall in the market, each in their winter coats, buttoned right up to the top, each with their

they sound old – my gran has a winter hat

felt <u>winter hats</u> on, Molly's in <u>pale green</u> and

depressing colour   *lighter/prettier than Theresa's*

Theresa's in <u>maroon</u>, but the girl in the white

overall had sliced through the pudding in an instant and Molly had been distracted by the marbled pattern of the sausage and the girl's

probably a black pudding is a kind of sausage

long, scarlet-painted fingernails. <u>Theresa's</u>

she sounds like she's got a suspicious nature

<u>lips were pursed distrustfully</u>, and her eyes

were <u>locked</u> on to the scales. *prisons have locks*

Later, Molly and Theresa had been

they don't drive

sitting on the <u>bus</u> on their way back home,

their shopping trolley with its square, black sides upright in the luggage compartment,

95

trolley is 'frozen' T's gaze is 'steely'=cold words
(I don't like Theresa)

frozen rigid with Theresa's steely gaze. Molly

wondered if now might be the time, but as she prepared herself to speak Theresa pointed out of the bus window at a disused cinema that had now become a children's activity centre. She reminded Molly that in their day, before the war, the back alleys were good enough for playing in. Molly nodded in agreement.

Now if she didn't say anything, she knew she never would. Molly knew she was timid – Theresa had told her often enough, and so had Charles – and her small amount of resolve was trickling through her fingers like fine sand. She watched her older sister, hands sheathed in oven gloves, lift the casserole onto the asbestos mat on the tray on the kitchen table tablecloth. Now, before she takes the lid off...

"I've been thinking of contacting Charles," said Molly.

"Contacting Charles!" Theresa was utterly incredulous. "But he's been dead for seven years!"

"Oh, I know you'll think I'm silly –"

I don't know what this means – agree? disagree? prob. agree as Molly gives in all the time

Molly laughed girlishly to concede this point,

↖ Molly acts young

"but Mrs Plumstead – Hettie's neighbour – she's a medium, you know, and they say she's very good. And she doesn't charge a lot – she does it because it's a gift, you see, and I didn't think it would do any harm... *↖ the way Molly talks makes*

her seem uncertain, scared of what T. will say

96

for her reaction

Molly watched her sister's face. She was quite impassive. Then she lowered her eyelids

help!

fractionally and formed her lips into a shape resembling a smile, but a smile so satirical that even the casserole dish seemed to quail in submission.

if the dish is frightened of her, she must be really scary!

"I'll be interested to see how you get on," she said.

weird - they are both old ladies! It's like T. is the boss here!

Molly was astonished. Did this mean she had permission?

"Can I?" she asked, knowing that it was

Molly thinks she's foolish

foolish for a woman of seventy-two to seek approval from her older sister for her actions, but unable to help herself. Molly had always been a good girl.

obedient

Theresa sniffed.

"You can do what you like. I'm surprised at you, Molly, believing all that twaddle."

this word shows T's contempt - but she hasn't stopped her going - is she curious?

97

This candidate has got the beginnings of a good answer. He's been very thorough and all that underlining will help him find examples to prove the points he needs to make. The next stage shows him making notes to answer the question.

<u>THERESA</u> – Older sister, bossy, fussy, suspicious of everyone, even objects are scared of her – the trolley is "frozen" and the casserole dish "quails". She's got her opinions and sticks to them (children playing). She looks down on Molly.

<u>MOLLY</u> – 72 but younger sister, widow. Wants to see a medium – obviously believes in that stuff. Shy of telling T. Keeps hesitating. She's obedient. Her coat's a lighter colour. She likes looking at things like the sausage & nails – like a child would. She agrees with T. It says in the passage she's timid. Her resolve trickles. Girlishly – like a child. She makes excuses for wanting to see the medium. A good girl.

<u>RELATIONSHIP</u> T very much the older sister, bossy, lays down the law. Puts her sister down. Molly gives in, like a child, but she still does what she wants. She seems like the nicer one, like she could have fun. M is scared of T, obedient, etc.

In an exam your notes would be a lot shorter than this and probably so messy that only you would know what they mean. You are working to time, after all. Making notes like this, under headings, helps you check you don't miss out any part of the question. You can use the notes as a guide when you start writing your answer.

A last word
Examiners like to surprise you, and it's never possible to predict what your passage will be about, or what the questions will be, even if you've been daft enough to study all the old GCSE English papers ever printed.

So the best advice possible is relax, don't worry, don't work too hard beforehand, and let yourself get really absorbed in the passage, while remembering all the advice in this section.

And read! Read anything you can get your hands on – books, papers, magazines, junk mail – the more used you are to reading and thinking about what you're reading, the easier comprehensions will become – I promise!

Quick!
I need a lit kit!

In this section you'll find everything you need to know about responding to literature in your English GCSE.

Most GCSE boards ask you to study literature as part of your coursework, so that you can have more time to really get into the texts. You might also have to study an anthology of texts, and be prepared to remember them and write about them under exam conditions. Either way, this section is essential reading.

You'll also be expected to show knowledge of both pre-twentieth century texts and twentieth century texts. This is because it's interesting to see how literature has changed over the years, both in the things people like to write about, and the language they use. Literature (and this section) is also conveniently divided into three different types, or if you want to use the jargon, *genres*. These are:

- Plays
- Prose (both short stories and novels)
- Poetry

The one writer who appears in every GCSE English syllabus is – you've guessed it – Shakespeare. We've a whole special section devoted to him. Plus we've got a Jargonbuster which will decode all the tricky lit terms you'll come across.

NOTE: For literature assignments with extra points-appeal, don't only read this section. Check out the sections on essay-writing on page 157 and coursework on page 202.

Shakespeare

You get asked enough questions on Shakespeare. Have you ever felt like asking him a few questions?

Yeah! I reckon he's overrated, right? You get better plots on the telly, no one except English teachers can even understand his plays, and I don't see why every student in the country has to study one of them for GCSE. Who is this guy?

Me – an ordinary bloke who lived mostly in London writing plays to make a living. I never realized they'd last so long. I'm quite flattered to think they're still being read and performed.

Except no one can understand them.

I can see what the problem is. The language has changed a lot in 400 years. When I wrote my plays everyone could follow them. Mind you, I still tried to put as much sex and violence in them as I could. Do you know *Romeo and Juliet?* Or *Macbeth?* And how about that pound of flesh in the *Merchant of Venice?* I can assure you, that kept bums on seats.

Yeah, but the other thing about your plays is that they're written in verse. No one spoke like that in real life – even 400 years ago. You're a bit of a poseur, aren't you?

102

Come on – give a guy a break! Everyone wrote plays in verse then. You had to, if you wanted to be taken seriously. Anyway, I don't write in verse all the time. Servants and comic characters talk in everyday sentences.

And that's another point I wanted to raise with you. None of your jokes are funny. No one laughs at them except English teachers and class swots.

People's sense of humour changes over the years too. It's got a lot to do with fashion. I can't help being born 400 years too early.

Yeah, but that's exactly my point. This is the twenty-first century. Why do we have to study old plays?

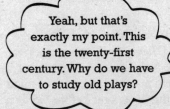

103

A good question. But maybe you have to study them first to find out.

He's a bit of a smartass, isn't he?

It's true – Shakespeare's plays *are* very difficult to read. If your teacher looks as if he understands them, it's only because he's studied them beforehand.

Shakespeare's plays were handed down to us in a number of different manuscripts – written by hand and occasionally indecipherable. So if sometimes the lines don't seem to make any sense – this could be because they really *don't* make sense, and no one, not even the best Shakespearian scholars, have been able to work out what they mean!

Nevertheless, here are some hints for getting the most out of Shakespeare's language:

- **Watch out for dead words**, which are words that we don't use any more. In *Romeo and Juliet*, Shakespeare uses the word "mammet". It means doll. Nobody can work that out without checking the glossary (dictionary) at the back of their book. Once you've done that, write the meaning of the word on top of the word in your edition of the play, so it's there to remind you.

104

- **If a word ends in "eth" substitute "s"**, so that "droppeth" becomes "drops".

- **Use the notes in your edition of the play** to help you understand the lines where Shakespeare plays around with the word order or misses words out (unfortunately, he does this a lot). For example, in *Macbeth*, Macbeth says 'To know my deed, 'twere best not know myself' just after he kills Duncan, the King of Scotland. What he meant was something like "If I really sat down and thought about what I've just done, it would make me hate myself so much I wouldn't want to know myself."

- **Read the lines aloud.** That makes the sense become clearer.

- **Best of all, SEE the play!** Shakespeare isn't sacred, and he isn't easy. But when you start to think about what his plays are actually about, they begin to feel relevant – and they are worth the effort.

Romeo and Juliet
A steamy tragedy about two under-age lovers who defy their parents and end up dead – includes fight scenes, drugs and dirty jokes.

Macbeth
A bloody power struggle, witchcraft, ghosts and brutal murder enacted on stage – but also a brilliant study of the nature of evil – all too relevant today.

The Merchant of Venice
Racism, greed and cross-dressing.

A Midsummer Night's Dream
Sex, mistaken identities, more sex and fairies!

Julius Caesar
Political life as you have never seen it before – makes today's politicians look squeaky-clean. And always read your horoscope before you go anywhere.

Plays

Much of the following advice about studying plays applies to Shakespeare's plays as well as to more modern drama.

WARNING

Whenever you write about a play, remember to refer to it as a PLAY and not as a "book". Nothing irritates examiners more than this.

When you read a play in class or by yourself, you've really only got half the product in front of you. The script of a play is a two-dimensional thing – the play performed on the stage is the three-dimensional thing. A playscript is to a play what a cake recipe is to a cake. Reading a recipe might give you a good idea of what the baked cake could be like, but you need to eat the cake to find out for sure. The same applies to a play – you need to see it (not eat it!).

Best of all, read the script *then* see the play!

- Plays are built round *characters*. It's a good idea to remember that the characters are invented by the playwright – they are not real people. There's no point in wondering what they did before the play begins because they didn't exist.

- Plays consist purely of *dialogue* (conversation between characters) and *stage directions* (instructions on the set, how characters should act, etc.).

- Plays are normally divided into acts, which are usually divided into scenes. Watch to see how the playwright or dramatist uses these divisions to create climaxes or suspense.

Studying a play

Read it, see it, talk about it to your mates and *make notes* on it.

That last part's easy. You can go to any bookshop and buy notes on your set texts and use them...

No, that's not the same thing. Commercial printed notes have to be used with extreme caution. They are quite useful if you don't properly understand a text, but *never* rely on them for your ideas. This is because your cunning examiner has read *all* the commercial notes and can recognize obvious borrowings.

So you mean I've got to come up with my own ideas?

That's right. And that's what making notes is all about.

A guide for making your own notes

- Keep a brief scene-by-scene *summary* of the play so you know where to find things later.

- Make a list of the *characters*, and for each write down the qualities you associate with them, noting down evidence.

- Think about the *themes* of the play (what the play is about) and say what you think the playwright thinks about them.

- If you've been set an assignment or question, *think about the question* as you read the play, and jot down any thoughts you have, noting down the section of the play that inspired them. (There's more help on doing this in the essay-writing section on page 157.)

- You might be studying a play in class – reading it with your teacher. If that's the case, don't think you'll just be able to remember all the clever things people say about the play – you'll need to have a system for writing down ideas that come up in discussion, so you can store them away for later.

Read on ... with these recommended plays:

An Inspector Calls	J B Priestley
Spring and Port Wine	Bill Naughton
A View from the Bridge	Arthur Miller
A Taste of Honey	Shelagh Delaney

Novels and short stories

So what is a novel? Is it the same thing as a book?

Not exactly. A book can be anything printed between hardback or paperback covers; a novel is a long, continuous story written in prose.

Run that word past me again?

Prose is just a catch-all name for anything that isn't written in verse. This book is in prose. Strictly speaking when you're writing about a novel you should call it a novel and not a book.

Pre-twentieth century novels

You might be asked to read a pre-twentieth century novel. Since the English novel only got going in the second half of the eighteenth century, this could easily mean a nineteenth-century, or Victorian novel.

In Victorian times, they didn't have the telly, and so people looked to novels to supply them with entertainment. So Victorian novels are very, very long. Victorian writers (such as Charlotte Bronte, who wrote *Jane Eyre*) reckoned people had lots of time to read, and filled their novels with lots of detailed descriptions of setting and feelings. To read a Victorian novel, you need patience – but you'll be rewarded by some of the best story-telling around – *Jane Eyre* includes madness, arson attempts, bigamy, cruelty to children and a red-hot love affair!

> The word "novel" comes from the Italian "novella" – meaning "tale" or "piece of news". Some early novels had really silly titles like *Humphry Clinker* and *Roderick Random*.

How to study a novel or short story

1. Read it from cover to cover, and enjoy.

2. Decide whether you liked it or not, and why. As the reader, you have rights too!

3. Remember that a novel is a made-up story by the novelist – it didn't really happen, though it may be based on real events. Consider all the different parts of the novel in turn. Use this checklist:

a) CHARACTERS
Who are the main characters?
What are they like?
How do you know what they're like?
(i.e. find evidence)

b) PLOT
What is the story?
How does it end?
How have the characters caused
the ending?

c) SETTING
Where is the novel set?
When is the novel set?
Is the setting important to the plot and characters?

d) THEMES
What ideas are examined in the novel?
(e.g. a *theme* of *Jane Eyre* is love)
What does the writer seem to think about these themes?
(This is a harder section but you can do it!)

e) THE WAY THE WRITER WRITES
Are there funny bits?
Does he or she use similes and metaphors a lot?
Do any passages stand out as memorable, and why?
Are there any parts which are full of suspense?

If you can answer most of these questions, you're well on your way to a brilliant study of your novel. Also consult the Plays section on page 108 to see how you could make notes on your novel.

There are many, many good novels to read, depending on your personal taste. You don't have to read a so-called classic just because everyone nags you to – reading any novel will help you with GCSE English. Check out what your mates are reading, look for book reviews in the magazines you read and join your local library. For starters, read on with these novels:

Jane Eyre	Charlotte Bronte
To Kill a Mockingbird	Harper Lee
Of Mice and Men	John Steinbeck
Kes	Barry Hines
Anita and Me	Meera Syal

SHORT STORIES are normally published in anthologies – ask your teacher for recommendations. Short stories are excellent for a quick, powerful read, and you can study them just as you would a novel. They tend to deal with a shorter time span than a novel, maybe even just one critical moment.

> What I like most about short stories is they're SHORT!

Poetry

> I hate poetry. It's, like, you read it, but there's no point. Nothing happens.

> I can never work out what a poem's supposed to be about. It's all right when the teacher goes over it, but by myself I don't understand a word.

112

Poetry is a bit like caviar in that...

No! It's like caviar in that you appreciate it more in small quantities, you should take it slowly, and then you'll find it contains some of the richest, most rewarding literature there is, only it's an acquired taste – you need practice to enjoy it.

OK. Do you like music?

Do you ever listen to the lyrics?

Do they mean anything to you?

Lyrics are poetry, only they're set to music. There's not a lot of space in a song to get your feelings across so you have to squeeze the language, getting rid of extra words, and you only include the words and images that matter. A poem is the same. It's because every word counts that poetry is both hard to understand, and brilliant when you do understand it. Or poetry is like painting with words. It's the overall effect that matters, not always the story.

Sadly a lot of people lose interest in poetry at school because teachers sometimes use poetry as tests, or over-analyse them. Poets write poetry because they're in the mood for writing a poem, and something has happened that makes them want to write. The last thing they want to do is give you grief. They want you to read or hear their poems and share in their mood or experience.

Advice for poetry-phobics.

1. Listen to your favourite song lyrics.
2. Read poetry by modern, funny poets like Roger McGough and John Hegley.
3. See if you can go to a poetry reading – poems are meant to be listened to.
4. Write your own poetry.

In Elizabethan times, it was cool to write a poem to your girlfriend to show her how much you fancied her. Even the most macho soldiers could write pretty good poetry!

On the plus side, poems are short, easy to remember and actually quite easy to write about – if you know what to look for.

What to look for in a poem

- **Words that stand out.** Poets are good at choosing just the right word, and it's fun to think in how many different ways that word is the right one. Sometimes it can be because of other words that the word reminds you of, or it might be just because of the sound of the word.

116

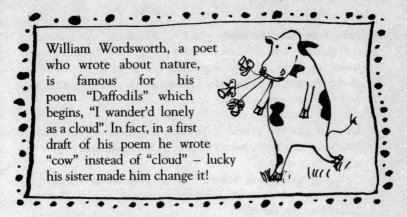

William Wordsworth, a poet who wrote about nature, is famous for his poem "Daffodils" which begins, "I wander'd lonely as a cloud". In fact, in a first draft of his poem he wrote "cow" instead of "cloud" – lucky his sister made him change it!

- **Similes and metaphors.** When a poet uses a comparison, he or she does so for a reason. You try to work out what the reason or reasons are.

- **The rhythm of the poem.** Ask yourself how it fits the subject matter. To tell if a poem's rhythm is fast or slow, see if you can work out whether the syllables are *long* or *short*. *Short* syllables (like cat, bed, if, dog, gun) have short vowel sounds that you can say quickly. *Long* syllables have long vowel sounds, such as double vowels (weed, moon) or the vowel sounds are the way we speak the vowels when we say the alphabet aloud (cave, leap, fire, toad, cute). Sad poems generally have lots of long, slow syllables, whereas cheerful poems have lots of short syllables. You could also check and see if the long and short syllables make a regular pattern.

- **Does the poem rhyme?** Poems don't need to rhyme, although most poets do create rules for themselves to follow if they're writing a poem – maybe they'll choose to write a sonnet (14 lines) or a ballad (short, rhyming verses). Or they'll decide, say, to have a very short second line in each verse. Why do you think your poet has decided to rhyme/not to rhyme? Why has he or she chosen their particular rules?

- **How does the poem make you feel?** Answering this question will guide you to the mood of the poem. How did the poem make you feel that way? Was it the choice of subject matter, or the way the subject matter is treated? You can write a funny poem about a sad subject.

- **Do you like the poem?** Examiners are always interested to hear your response. Always include it, but make sure you have a good reason for it.

    Example of a *good* reason: "The language used to describe the horses makes me feel sorry for them and the slow rhythm underlines the sad effect."

    Example of a *bad* reason: "My Dad wrote it, and he'd kill me if I said I didn't like it."

    What if you didn't like the poem? It's OK to say you didn't like it, but *never* say "because it's boring" (which is the worst thing you could possibly write). Try to explain what your problem is with the poem very carefully – for example, "It was too sad and there was so much emotion I felt like I didn't want to carry on reading." *Don't* say "because I didn't understand it" (even if you didn't) – it makes you sound as if you haven't tried.

There are several ways you might end up reading poems in your English GCSE. Some of you will have anthologies of poetry to study in class, or you might write a coursework assignment on several poems on the same theme, or several poems by the same poet. Or you might even have an exam where you're given a poem you've not read before and have to answer questions on it. Whichever is the case for you, the above guidelines on what to look for in poetry will keep your head above water.

The jargon buster
Every business has its own jargon. For example:

The business of literature is no different. To be able to write well about literature you need to know the jargon, and use it. Examiners will reward you for it.

SIMILE = a comparison using "like" or "as".

METAPHOR = a comparison that doesn't use "like" or "as".

IMAGERY = a collective name for similes and metaphors.

DICTION = a writer's choice of words.

PERSONIFICATION = giving a non-human thing human qualities.

PATHETIC FALLACY = usually making the weather in a text match the mood of the main character.

IRONY = when a writer says one thing but deliberately means the opposite, a bit like sarcasm.

DRAMATIC IRONY = when the audience knows more than the characters on the stage.

ALLITERATION = words close to each other beginning with the same sound (and usually the same initial letter).

121

SOLILOQUY = a speech in a play spoken by a character alone on the stage to reveal his thoughts and feelings.

THEME = the subject (often abstract) of a text, the ideas in it.

ATMOSPHERE = the feeling a passage gives you.

TONE = the attitude of the writer towards his or her material.

BLANK VERSE = verse that has about 10 syllables per line and a regular rhythm but doesn't rhyme.

CONTRAST = two very different things placed very near to each other.

122

How do you write right in English?

In both your exams and your coursework folder, you'll be expected to show you can write in a variety of ways...

Such as standing on my head, or balancing on one leg?

I'll ignore that. Some boards will want you to do some creative writing, such as stories, or you might be asked to write a description, or to try some personal writing. Not only that, but you might need to write an essay, or construct an argument, write a letter, report, newspaper article, or the text for an advertisement, or anything the examiner fancies.

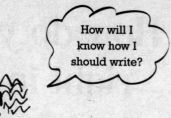

How will I
know how I
should write?

By reading this section thoroughly.

This section is divided into three:

1. NON-LITERARY FORMS OF WRITING:
    letters
    reports
    newspaper articles
    reviews
    posters, leaflets and flyers
    constructing an argument
    being persuasive
    analysing, reviewing and commenting

2. LITERARY FORMS OF WRITING:
    narrative writing
    personal writing
    descriptive writing
    empathetic writing
    playscripts

3. HOW TO WRITE AN ESSAY

Feel free to read these sections in any order which appeals to you!

124

Non-literary forms of writing

There are three golden rules that apply to all the kinds of writing in this section:

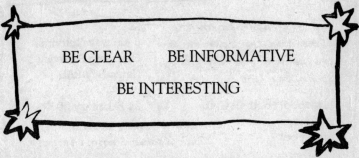

BE CLEAR   BE INFORMATIVE

BE INTERESTING

Being clear is all about writing correct English, ordering what you have to say in a logical manner, and looking at what you have written from the reader's point of view.

Being informative is about checking you have enough useful and interesting detail.

Being interesting is all about putting yourself in the reader's shoes and including devices to keep the reader's attention.

In fact, one of the best ways you can prepare yourself for any practical piece of writing is to ask yourself – *Who am I writing this FOR?* Forget about your English teacher. Instead you must work out who your intended imaginary *audience* is. It could be the readers of a newspaper, it might be members of a town council, it might be an elderly person – read carefully the task that you've been set, identify your imaginary audience, and write deliberately for it.

Next, you must look carefully at the form you've been asked to write in. Each form of writing has its own rules. Just as it's possible to write down the rules of, say, a sport, it's possible to lay down rules for different sorts of writing.

Letters

For writing a formal or business letter, follow these rules.

put your address on the right and the address of the person you're writing to on the left

5 Railway Cuttings,
Chipping Sadbury,
Hants HT7 8AB

Liverpool Football Club,
Anfield,
Liverpool

24 February 2000

leave a space between your address and the date

leave another space here

Dear Sir,

It is with extreme regret that I turn down the proposal of marriage you have forwarded to me from Michael Owen.

I have nothing but the greatest admiration for Mr Owen, but have to inform you that I am already going out with Wayne Evans, my boyfriend for the last two years.

I do hope Michael will not be too disappointed, and that he finds happiness elsewhere.

Yours faithfully,

Angela Jackson

leave a space between the ending and your name

Angela Jackson

126

- Begin:
  Dear Sir, if you don't know the name of the person and you're sure it's a he;
  Dear Madam, if you don't know the name of the person and you're sure it's a she;
  Dear Sir or Madam, if you don't know the name of the person and you want to hedge your bets;
  or *Dear Mr* or *Dear Mrs* or *Dear Ms* or *Dear Miss* followed by surname.
  It's not advisable to address someone by their first name in a business letter, unless you know them socially.

- Set out your letter in brief paragraphs using formal English – never any slang.

- Make sure the purpose of the letter is crystal-clear.

- End as follows:
  Letters starting *Dear Sir or Madam* ... *Yours faithfully*
  Letters starting *Dear Mr or Mrs Surname* ... *Yours sincerely*
  Note that some people find the spelling of "sincerely" rather tricky, so make a point of remembering it and getting it right. Also "faithfully" and "sincerely" never have capital letters (and "yours" doesn't have an apostrophe).

E-mails haven't replaced letters for everything yet, and you might find there are times when you can't even get on a computer. In which case, it's back to letter-writing.

Reports

And we don't mean a school report! You might be asked to produce a straightforward, factual piece of writing *reporting* on a set of circumstances, or explaining something in your own words that you have just read.

When writing a report, the most important thing is to be clear. You must arrange material in a logical order, if necessary using sub-headings. As always, bear your imaginary audience in mind.

POLICE REPORT OF INCIDENT AT OAKLANDS COURT, NEWTOWN

I entered the flat at 7.35 p.m. There were signs of habitation but no-one was present. The corpse was lying slightly to the left of the radiator.

- The head had been severed and could not be found.
- The intestines had been arranged into a coil outside the corpse.
- No murder weapons were visible.

Immediately I contacted the forensic department, but as I dialled the number I heard movement inside the flat. I apprehended the intruder and his interest in the corpse persuaded me he was the perpetrator. I took his personal details.

- Name – "Snowy" Watkins
- Age – 5
- Appearance – white, long-haired, with patches of tabby

I gave the remains of the mouse a decent burial.

128

Let's face it, writing reports isn't the most exciting activity you can think of, and (dare we say it?) sometimes the examiners lack a little bit of imagination when it comes to setting you juicy subjects. It's just possible that you'll be faced with a subject that you care little about, and know less…

Write a report for the town council on ways of improving the environment of your home town.

A leaden feeling of despair envelops you. On the bus in the morning you're too tired to notice your environment, and on the way home from school you're too busy chatting with your mates. The only bit of town you're familiar with is the shopping centre – how on earth do you know what needs improving in your home town?

1. Time to use a little imagination. Remember the examiner is less interested in the truth than in your way of writing.

You can pretend you live in a town with a really cheesy environment, and then set about writing a report about ways to improve it. (Probably unwise to let your imagination take over completely and write your report on your environment in a Martian space station.)

2. Develop ideas using a spidergram.

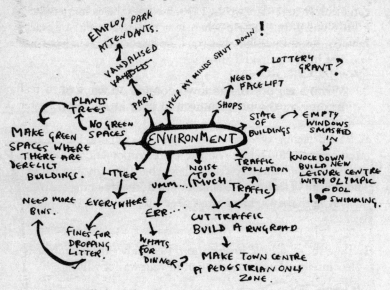

If you still don't have enough material, take each final label from your spidergram, make a subtitle of it, and write examples below.

If you then write a few sentences on each label and each example, you'll have plenty of material.

This kind of writing is what is meant when you're asked to INFORM, EXPLAIN and DESCRIBE. You introduce facts clearly, with examples. Watch out for those three key words appearing on your exam papers.

> **TOP TIP**
> It's always a good idea to go into as much detail as possible in these sorts of questions.

Newspaper articles

How do you go about these? Who better to ask than a real journalist – Sarah Lester, who is a reporter for the Manchester Evening News.

Is there an art to writing good newspaper articles?

Yes, definitely. What you write has to be clear, and you've got to grab your reader straight away. Also, there's got to be a logic to your thought processes. As you write, you've got to answer the questions that would be in the reader's mind, as they occur to him or her. Say there was an explosion. The questions would be – Was anyone hurt? Who? Where was the explosion? etc.

Any tips for aspiring journalists?

If you're reporting a story, imagine you are telling someone, or having a conversation with them. This will help you prioritize the important facts in the story. Also you should put in first the details that affect people, not the boring old facts. Readers are always interested in people – oh, and dogs!

You've always got to use simple, clear language that anyone could understand. It also helps to write in short sentences.

131

Would you go about writing a report and a feature differently?

Yes. A report is shorter and more disciplined – you've basically got to cut out all the unnecessary words. In a feature you can have more fun. There's a more flexible word limit, you can use longer sentences, more descriptive detail and you can even be flowery.

If you're asked to write a *newspaper report*, always:

1. Write in complete sentences.

2. Leave out subtitles.

3. Make your first sentence say exactly what the report is about.

4. Use straightforward language. You might also like to include brief quotations from people involved.

This week's rollover Lottery winner is from Anytown – and he's only 16! Richard Black, of Hyde Road, Anytown, has won £6,750,000 with a ticket he bought on his 16th birthday. "I'm over the moon," Richard said. "I'm going to invest in a new house, a fleet of Mercedes and a designer wardrobe. Then I'm flying round the world – that is, after I've done my GCSEs."

A *newspaper feature* is generally longer, has more local colour, humour, description – whatever you feel is appropriate.

Reviews

- Describe the thing you are reviewing concisely.

- Give your opinion on it – with reasons.

- Write as if you are addressing someone who hasn't read/seen/been to the thing you are reviewing, and you're helping them decide whether it's worthwhile.

Posters, leaflets and flyers

- Plan the layout before you begin.

- Don't waste too much time on artwork – you'll be assessed only on your writing.

- Be very tidy – if you are designing a leaflet for coursework, you might think about using a computer.

- Don't use too few words. A leaflet will get a low mark if there isn't enough there to mark! Use enough words to demonstrate your new-found skills.

- Make a special effort with spelling and punctuation. Nothing looks worse than a spelling error in a headline. It shouts:

Now that we've looked at some common forms of non-literary writing, we'll move on to some more *techniques* that you'll need to use.

Constructing an argument

I think we might have a different idea about what an argument is. You think it's a fight; I think it's expressing an opinion with reasons.

Not so. It feels good to make a case for something you believe in – and useful too. It's not too difficult, either. You might need to construct an argument in one of several situations. You might be asked to give your opinion on an issue, such as smoking in public places, in an essay. You might have to read a passage or two passages, and using them, give your opinion on the contents, and say which one you agree with. You might be asked to give your opinion in the form of a letter or a newspaper article. Some boards are very helpful, and actually highlight the word "argue" in the question – so there's no argument!

Sometimes the subject you're asked to write about might be quite interesting to you, or you'll feel strongly about it. Then you'll find it easy to find things to say.

But what if you don't? Then develop ideas using the spidergram technique on page 130.

Make sure you don't fall into the trap of stating your opinion without reasons. It's never enough just to say, for example, "It's wrong to allow smoking in public places." That's an assertion (a statement of what you believe). It's not an argument – an argument is an assertion plus reasons to back it up.

To construct an argument you need to go down to the pet shop and purchase a WHY parrot. When you are arguing in an essay, speech or letter, allow it to perch on your shoulder and squawk "WHY?!"

For example:

It's wrong to allow smoking in public places.

Because passive smoking is bad for people's health.

Particles of smoke can lodge in your lungs even if it's not you who's smoking, and they can cause respiratory problems.

(Your WHY parrot is quiet now. You can begin again.)

It's not fair for smokers to smoke in public places.

Anyone can go to a public place.

WHADD'YA MEAN BY A PUBLIC PLACE? SPELL IT OUT, WHY DON'CHA?

(Your WHY parrot's getting cheeky.)

A public place could be a cinema, restaurant, shop, bar, theatre, bingo hall.

ALL RIGHT - I GET THE PICTURE.

It's not fair for smokers to smoke in these places.

Non-smokers should not be forced to inhale other people's smoke.

WHY, WHY, WHY????!!!

Non-smokers should have the freedom to pursue a healthy lifestyle.

136

WHAT ABOUT SMOKERS? DON'T THEY HAVE RIGHTS?

(Your WHY parrot is a real smartass.)

They do have rights, but they shouldn't be allowed to restrict the rights of others, which is what they do when they smoke in a public place.

BUT WHAT IF THERE'S A SMOKERS' AREA?

That's better. But smoke can waft over from a smokers' area, and pollute the non-smokers' area.

I THINK YOU'RE EXAGGERATING THE RISKS OF PASSIVE SMOKING.

Look at these statistics...

(Your parrot interrupts with a rather nasty smoker's cough...)

As you can see here, first you've got to provide plenty of reasons and examples for your argument, and also try to pre-empt the other side of the argument by meeting their objections before they can make them! For example, *I know you think two o'clock is too late to come home but I don't have school in the morning...*

Being persuasive

To a large extent, being persuasive is the same thing as arguing. When you're persuading someone, you are trying to win him or her over to your point of view. So again you need to give your opinion, then state your reasons.

However, you might be asked to write something like a speech, or text for an advertisement. In these cases it's a good idea to spice up your arguments with hard-hitting expression. Look at this example.

> So in conclusion I beg you to vote for the Freedom at Fifteen party in the forthcoming election. Remember: we are the only party which will ban homework, pay school students a decent living wage of £30,000 per annum, and make it compulsory for teachers to wear school uniform. With our exciting manifesto, could you even consider voting for anyone else? Moreover, together we can fight for free admission to football matches and rock concerts, and introduce GCSEs in Partying and Fashion Sense. For centuries young people have been oppressed by hypocritical and contradictory parents; this must stop, and it must stop now!

Did you spot the following cunning techniques?
- rhetorical questions (questions which don't expect an answer, like "could you even consider voting for anyone else?")
- hard facts which in this case act as bribes (wages for students, no homework, etc.)
- addressing audience as "you" (to be chummy) and as "we" to include the reader
- emotive language ("fight for", "oppressed")
- exaggeration ("For centuries young people have been oppressed...")

Look carefully at the wording of your writing task, and if you think a little bit of persuasion is called for, nick some of these techniques.

Analysing, reviewing and commenting

This is the sort of writing where you home in on detail and weigh it up. You are most likely to do this in an essay-style task, so if you want help with analysing, evaluating or reviewing, move straight to the essay-writing sub-section on page 157.

Literary forms of writing

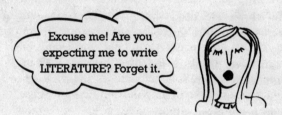

Literature is only a word for stories – in fact, the word literature can just mean "things which are written". Some boards might ask you to do some *creative writing*, and this section will help you prepare for that.

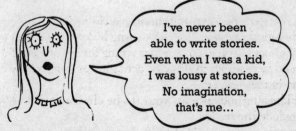

Everyone has an imagination; what you suffer from is a lack of confidence.

139

Try this quiz to identify the sort of writer you are. Tick the box by the statements that apply most closely to you.

1. I've got no imagination – I can never think of ideas for stories. ☐

2. My stories always wander off the point. ☐

3. I have plenty of ideas, but they're all rubbish. ☐

4. My stories are dead short – I run out of things to say. ☐

5. I can never think of the first sentence of a story. ☐

6. I can never bring my stories to an end. ☐

7. My stories are so boring even I wouldn't want to read them. ☐

8. If I get a list of titles, I can never decide which one to write about. ☐

9. My life is so boring – that's why I can't think of ideas for stories. ☐

If you ticked 3, 8 or 9 – you're an INDECISIVE WRITER.
If you ticked 1, 4 or 5 – you're a CONSTIPATED WRITER.
If you ticked 2, 6, or 7 – you're a FREE-FALL WRITER.

Help is at hand for all three sorts of writers, but there's nothing to stop you picking up tips from all three sections. And remember, whichever section you choose, you should go on to page 148 for advice which applies to everyone.

Help for indecisive writers

You're the sort of person who spends more time thinking about what to write than writing it. You're the one whose mind is an utter blank, or changes more times than a model during a fashion shoot. And just when you've finally decided what to write about, your time is up…

So what can you do about it?

Indecisive writers often lack confidence. Just remind yourself that everyone can tell a story. It's what you do when you tell your mates about the match last night, or the party last Saturday. It's what you do when you lie in bed daydreaming about winning an Olympic medal or the lottery. Everyone has an imagination, and yours is unique. Whatever you write is going to be just that bit different from everyone else's writing. What seems obvious to you might seem like a brilliant thought to the person who hasn't thought of it!

First of all, work out what sort of writing you do best:

- Stories – where you make up events, maybe with a twist in the tale.
- Chatty writing, where you interest someone with funny or moving accounts of your life.

141

- Descriptive writing, where you set a scene or an atmosphere, or even introduce a person.

By looking back over your past work, you should be able to decide where your talents lie. Then, if you have to do some creative writing either for coursework or in an exam, you know which sort to commit yourself to.

Once you're committed, and you have a title, you have to decide what to write about.

Do this by **brainstorming**:

Write down your title and underneath it put as many ideas as possible for something you could write. It doesn't matter how crazy they are at this stage.

LOST
- City lost against United
- a kid getting lost in the supermarket
- I lost my trainers last night
- losing your mind completely
- losing weight
- losing your way in a forest and meeting a vampire

Now you read through your list and decide which storyline has the most potential, bearing in mind the sort of writing you're best at. For example, if you like writing about football, a story based on your real-life experiences at the match might be a good idea. If you've got a good sense of humour, a funny story about losing your trainers or some weight might be OK. If you read nothing but horror stories in your spare time, then go for the vampire idea, as you probably know your stuff. If you like empathizing with other people's feelings, try the kid lost in the supermarket. The hardest title on this list is probably the one about losing your mind, as not many of us have had that experience, and so our stories are likely to feel a bit second-hand.

> **TOP TIP**
> Always try to set your stories somewhere familiar. If you
> don't, all your background details will be wrong, and your
> reader won't believe in your story.

Once you have your idea, then you must make a plan.

> Boring! Isn't the point
> about stories that you just
> go with the flow? If you're
> making it all up it doesn't
> matter about planning…

Unfortunately, no. It's precisely because you are making it all up
that you need to plan. Otherwise you really will get lost. But the
good news is that it doesn't take more than a few moments to
plan a story – read the section on planning under the advice for
free-fall writers on page 146.

A last word to indecisive writers. If you always get stuck on
the first sentence, then leave it out completely. Start with the
second sentence, or even the third, or even the next paragraph,
then go back at the end to your beginning. You'll find it a lot
easier then to start your story. Or you might even discover that
your second sentence IS your first sentence!

143

Help for constipated writers

Constipated writers can't get it to come out – the ideas, that is. They're the ones who think they have no imagination. They feel stuck all the time. Sometimes they think that they are the only ones who don't find it easy to come up with ideas for writing. Not true.

William Shakespeare, arguably the world's greatest playwright, stole 90 per cent of the stories for his plays. He rarely made his plots up, but nicked them from history books and other people's writing – and it didn't do him any harm.

So where can you **steal** stories from?

1. Your own life

You can write about anything that's happened to you in real life and pretend it's a story. Did you go pot-holing for the first time recently? Use that. Were you in the car when your mum got a speeding fine? Use that, but don't show her the story. Absolutely anything that happens to you can be turned into a story, and you're free to change bits, exaggerate here and there, and generally just make it a bit better than life.

2. The telly

Soaps, police and hospital dramas have some excellent stories in them, as I'm sure you know. Can you use them? Yes, but with a word of warning. You've got to change the stories a lot more than if you were using your own life. Examiners watch TV too, and they will recognize last week's episode of Coronation Street. But if one of the plot lines interests you, and you want to use that story to see what it would feel like if it happened to you, that's OK. Take the story and apply it to your life.

3. Magazines and newspapers

Get into the habit of reading all the weird and wonderful stories you find in the newspapers ("Woman married octopus in Guatemala"). Try turning some of these into stories, or imagine yourself in the position of one of the people in these stories.

4. Gossip

I bet your friends tell you some pretty fascinating things. I know you promised you'd never tell a soul about the time your friend's swimming cozzie slid off in the pool and he had to wait until everyone had gone before getting out, but all's fair in love, war and GCSEs. Just make sure you change the names!

Now you've stolen your idea, you need to get a plan – read the section on planning your story on page 146.

Help for free-fall writers

You're the sort of writer who has no problem beginning, who can chat away merrily, and write on and on and on, but you tend to fall to earth with a bump when you realize you can't end your story because it isn't going anywhere, or that you've repeated yourself, or that now you look at it it hardly makes any sense at all…

The antidote to being a free-fall writer is to **plan**. Planning is vital for all forms of writing. In fact, planning is vital for just about every activity, whether it's shopping in town for an outfit, or winning the match, or just a night in front of the telly with your family. Planning stops you running into problems, and makes it easier for you to get where you're going. If you don't plan to fail, don't fail to plan.

How to plan

1. Think of the end of your story first. It acts as a destination and stops you getting lost. It also means you can create suspense by hinting about the ending, or even hinting that the ending's going to be the opposite of what it is, thus surprising your reader.

2. Make out a list of the stages of your story. If you can only think of two or three stages, start breaking down the stages into sub-stages. Look at this example.

A story about a disastrous date...

The end:
I get food poisoning and come out in big red blotches at the meal.

Stages:
I fancy Joe, I let him know I fancy him, he asks me out, I'm dead nervous, it all goes wrong.

Sub-stages:
I fancy Joe – describe me, describe him, say who he is.

I let him know I fancy him – how I make sure he overhears me telling my mate I fancy him.

He asks me out – after swimming, when I look a mess, how thrilled I am.

I'm dead nervous – my feelings getting ready, explaining he's taking me out for dinner 'cos he's rich, feeling awkward in posh clothes as I only ever wear jeans.

It all goes wrong – we collide in the door going into the restaurant, I don't know which knives and forks to use, I have a drink and I get giggly, he looks embarrassed, then I eat some seafood, I start feeling sick and coming out in blotches, they have to call an ambulance, Joe is embarrassed to be seen with me but the paramedic is drop-dead gorgeous...

WARNING

Examiners have to plough through lots of romantic stories, so if you plan to write one make sure it's a good one!

Notice how the bulk of the detail is in the last section because the story is meant to be about the date itself. It's as well to spend as short a time as possible on the preliminaries and get straight down to the nitty-gritty. Otherwise, you could be accused of being irrelevant.

It's not what you say, it's the way that you say it

Free-fall writers, and all sorts of writers, need to read this section, which is about *how* you write. In fact, you can never give enough thought to how you write, because it's your style that will win you the most marks, not your ideas.

So, for top writing, try to:

- keep your reader's interest
- use appropriate words
- experiment with language for artistic effect

Keeping your reader's interest

1. Let your reader know that *you* know what the ending of your story will be.

2. Pick up on a detail or two that reveals character or setting really vividly.

3. Avoid pointless repetition … avoid pointless repetition … avoid pointless repetition – yes, we get it!

4. Use paragraphs to give your story structure. Work out the best order for your paragraphs so there is a logical flow to your writing, and the reader knows whether he's at the beginning, the middle or the end.

Using appropriate words and experimenting with language

This is what good writing is all about. Words are to writers as paint is to artists and notes are to musicians. Words are your raw material. The more varied and interesting your selection of words, the better your writing will be. Of course, your words have to fit the subject you're writing about.

Take the word WALK. There's more than one word which means nearly the same as walk. How many can you think of?

Give yourself two points for every word you thought of which is in the list below, and three (yes! three!) points for every word you thought of which isn't in the list – as long as it really is a sort of walking!

A score of 6 or more shows you that you can usually think of an alternative to a plain, old, boring word.

(**Answers:** stroll, saunter, amble, stagger, hobble, wander, stumble, proceed, march, stride)

Do not use long, complicated words in a vain attempt to impress the examiner if you're not 100 per cent certain what they mean – and don't make words up, either.

The best word is always the more accurate word, not the longest.

Q. Can I use slang?
A. Only if you're writing dialogue and your characters would normally use slang – otherwise avoid it.

Q. What words are slang?

A. Generally, a slang word is a perfectly good word used in the wrong situation, e.g. "cool" is the right word to use about an autumn's day, but slang when used about a film. Other words commonly used as slang include wicked, mean, really, dead (as in "dead smart"), brilliant, incredibly, fantastic – and these are only a selection!

Q. Why do I keep on getting told off about using the word "nice"?

A. It's not a very effective word because its meaning is vague, like "good". Try to substitute a more precise word

    nice day = warm, sunny day
    good dinner = tasty dinner
    nice person = warm-hearted and interesting person
    nice time = enjoyable time
    good book = absorbing book

Q. What if I need to use swear words in my story?

A. Even if your character might use swear words in real life, it's better for you *not* to use them. The last thing you want to do is upset your examiner – he or she might be a sensitive soul.

150

Top tips to spice up your writing

- Why not try adding some well-chosen detail to your writing, especially if you're finding it hard to think of different words? A detail can often bring a description or character in a story to life.

- Whoever is marking your story cannot fail to be impressed by sentences of varying lengths – it guarantees your writing won't be monotonous.

- Pick one, two, three or more of your five senses, and describe something in your story from that point of view – don't just see rain, but feel it and hear it. Don't just taste food, but smell it.

- Read as much as you can. Steal other writers' tricks for making their writing interesting. Let yourself be influenced by the style of your fave writers.

- If you meet a new word in a book or magazine, find out what it means, then use it. Adopt it and make it your own.

- Don't be afraid of using similes and metaphors in your writing. A well-chosen simile or metaphor really does bring writing to life.

- Always include thoughts and feelings in stories, so the reader feels close to the action.

151

Creative coursework

If you're working on creative writing for coursework, why don't you…

> …read your writing aloud to yourself (or the cat)? Is your meaning always clear? Is there a better word you could have used?
>
> …ask someone else (not the cat) to read your writing, and ask them for constructive comments?

Well, thanks for your help!

> …leave it for a day or two? Then try writing again, when you're more familiar with your story – second attempts are often better than first attempts.

Getting person-al

Before you start any piece of creative writing you have one important decision to make – which *person* are you going to write it in? Are you going to use the *first* person (I) or the *third* person (he/she)?

Bear in mind:

- Using the **first person** is essential for personal writing. In stories it helps you get closer to the thoughts and feelings of the central character.

- Using the **third person** is a more detached way of telling a story. It allows you – the author – to get inside the head of more than one character.

Different types of creative writing

Sometimes you might be instructed to write in a certain form:

- a story or narrative
- personal writing
- a description
- writing as a character from a passage (empathetic writing)
- a playscript

Just as with non-literary forms of writing, you need to be clear about what each form entails. So we'll run through them.

Narrative writing (stories)

Provided you have a simple plot, one or two interesting characters and lots of thoughts and feelings – and as long as you follow all the advice in this section! – you'll be fine.

Personal writing

This is where you are asked to write about yourself. In an exam, you might pick a title such as "My Ambitions", "An Evening I Will Never Forget", or "A Family Occasion". Write in the first person, use lots of detail, and if the truth isn't very interesting, lie!

You still need to plan personal writing, and follow all the tips above.

Good personal writing will make a reader smile, or tug at their heartstrings, or make the examiner feel that he or she would really like to get to know you – but then, would you really like to get to know an examiner?

Descriptive writing

Some boards will ask you to DESCRIBE a place you know well. Seems easy. All you have to do is conjure up the place, and let your pen do the talking. Just make sure you don't fall into these traps…

- **Going off the point.** Sometimes it's tempting to start telling a story that happened in the place, because a story seems more interesting than a description. Don't do it! If you've been asked to describe, just describe.

- **Writer's block.** This is where you can't bring the place to your mind at all. No sweat. Just make it up.

- **Not writing in sentences.** Sometimes in a description you find yourself doing this: "Children swinging on the swings. Toddlers playing in the sand-pit. Parents reading newspapers on the benches." Can you see what's wrong here? These aren't complete sentences – they have no main verbs. It should read, "Children *were* swinging on he swings."

- **Changing tenses in the middle.** You might start your description in the present tense, then find that you've switched to the past tense. Oh no you don't! In a description you've got to choose one tense and stick with it. Check your description to make sure you've not fallen into this common trap.

Empathetic writing

Empathetic writing is a posh way of saying the sort of writing where you pretend to *be* a character in a passage you've just read, or a text you know. Think of it as role-play – but on paper, not in your drama lesson, so less embarrassing.

154

Examiners who ask for empathetic writing are being extra-cunning. They want you to *both* write creatively *and* show you understood the text. Cheeky, aren't they?

Good empathy writing:

- refers to the details in the text and might use them in clever ways

- is when you become the character, express their thoughts and feelings rather than yours, and best of all, use the language the character would use themselves

- is always in the first person.

What? You mean if I had to be a dog, I would write, "I wagged my tail excitedly as I heard the postman come up the drive. I scampered up to the letterbox and waited, panting big, smelly breaths. Then as soon as his hand came through the door, I bit it!"

Not bad at all! You seem to have picked up quite a lot in this section. I like the unusual verbs like "scampered", the detail about the smelly breath, and your use of hearing.

Playscripts

There are a few brief rules about layout.

1. Write out the name of the speaker in capitals and follow with a colon.

2. Write out the speech without quotation marks.

3. You can include stage directions in brackets.

4. If the location changes, then start a new scene.

5. Make the dialogue natural sounding, but don't include every "um" and "er".

Scene 1: The classroom
ME: Here's my story, Sir.
TEACHER: Let me just have a look at it. (Reads.) I don't believe it! This is excellent! Superb! Worthy of publication! I'm proud to know you! (Grovels.)
ME: Thanks. You can stop grovelling now!

How to write an essay

The strict definition of an essay would be: an attempt at a literary composition on any subject.

In effect, yes. A piece of writing. At GCSE you might be asked to write an essay:

- in an exam
- for coursework
- about a literary text or texts
- about a non-literary subject, e.g. capital punishment.

So it'll pay to read this guide to essay-writing.

157

Whatever sort of essay you have to write, and whether it's for your coursework folder or done in an exam, there are some rules that always apply, just as there are rules that apply when you get dressed in the morning, although there are differences...

1. Begin by putting on your underwear – jazzy underwear can cheer you up in the morning – just make sure you cover the essentials!

1. *Begin with your* **introduction** *– thought-provoking, interesting and relevant to the title, making sure you cover the essentials.*

2. If it's a school day you ought to wear your uniform, or if your school doesn't have a strict uniform, put on something sensible you can work in.

2. *Use* **sensible, formal English**, *plain, clear and to the point – and if it's an essay about literature you can use a few literary terms (see page 120).*

3. School uniform alone is boring; personalise it by wearing your shirt out of your trousers, or maybe sneaking in an earring or two.

3. *A series of points in an essay is boring without **interesting detail**. Sneak them in to prove you're an individual, and to give your essay weight.*

4. Obviously you'll dress in a logical order; underwear then bottoms, top then sweater.

4. *Order your essay logically by writing in **paragraphs**. Cover one major point or two or three smaller, related points in each paragraph.*

5. Finish by checking yourself in the mirror, full-length, if possible, and look at the overall effect. Smile, and resolve to make a good impression on everyone you meet.

5. *Finish with a **conclusion**; a strong, interesting one as it will be the final impression the reader receives of you. And the reader will be the examiner…*

The following is a flowchart for you to follow and diagnose your essay-writing personality. When you've done that, you'll know which of the subsequent parts of this section apply most closely to you. But if I were you, I'd read them all anyway!

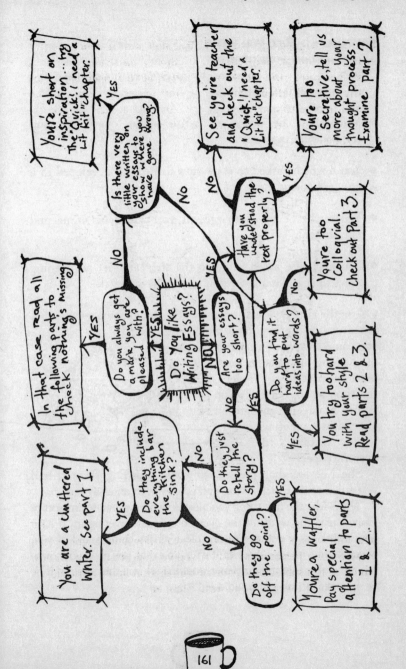

Part one – before you write
a) Get to know your question

Whenever you write an essay, it's in response to a question or a task. These are usually specific.

- You might be asked to write about characters and relationships in a novel.

- You might be asked to show how a theme is developed in a group of poems.

- You might be asked to present your views on crime and punishment.

- You might be asked to go to the shop and get an evening newspaper and a quarter pound of mint imperials...

OK, so the last one wasn't an essay title. But imagine if your mum asked you to do that. How would she react if you came back with a quarter pound of evening newspapers and a mint imperial, or never went to the shop at all, but ended up at Aunty Maureen's and ate all of her mint imperials while reading the evening paper?

She'd be less than pleased, as would your English teacher if you failed to do exactly what's asked of you in an essay task.

That's why the first thing you must do when you write any sort of essay is read the words of the *question* over and over again. If it's a coursework essay and you're not clear what's being asked of you, check it out with your teacher. If it's in an exam, you're on your own, but remember that the examiner wouldn't ask you the question if he or she didn't think you could do it.

A good idea is to underline the key words of the task so they are fixed in your mind. Even when you've read the question sufficiently and feel sure you know what's being asked of you, remember to look at it from time to time during the essay-writing process to make sure you haven't deviated from it, and are covering all parts of the question.

Putting in lots of material that doesn't answer the question is a waste of time, and can irritate your reader – remind yourself of this by checking out page 72.

However brilliant your ideas are – even if leading Shakespearian scholars regularly beat a path to your door, or the government are constantly pestering you to help them form policy – if you don't answer the question, you're a non-starter when it comes to essays.

TOP TIP
Teachers and examiners aren't as bright as you think they are!

They won't realize that you're answering the question unless you make it obvious to them. Make a point, then *link* it to the words of the question. Acknowledge the question in your introduction, refer to the question at the beginning of each paragraph, and answer the question finally in your conclusion. Then the poor old dears might twig that you're actually doing what is being asked.

In fact, why don't you assist the examiner still more by both putting the number of the question on your paper *and* writing out the title?

Like they say, help the aged.

b) Planning

So you've read the question so well you know it off by heart. Good.

Now you have to *plan* your answer. To refresh yourself on the importance of planning, sneak a peek at the planning section on page 146.

Whatever kind of writing you've embarked on, you must plan. In coursework you can take your time planning; in an exam you do it quickly – but do it!

Scoop!

This book is delighted to bring to you the typescript of the award-winning wildlife documentary "The lesser spotted essay-writer at work" as premiered on the National Naturewatch Cable and Satellite channel.

Welcome, viewers, to the living room of the lesser spotted essay-writer. I'm speaking in a hushed voice as I do not wish to startle the essay-writer, who you can see absorbed in thought. We have cameras hidden at strategic places in the room so we can pick up the creature's every move.

Look how it twiddles with its hair while staring at the question. Years of evolution have helped it develop this calming behaviour. Knowing the difficulty of the task ahead, the essay-writer reaches for a Jammy Dodger from the plate on the table and munches it. An essay-writer needs to consume at least 50,000 calories to maintain efficiency during the task ahead.

Note also the television screen in the corner, which is blank. Lesser spotted essay-writers generally need two to three hours of TV viewing a night in order to survive, but this essay-writer knows that the best essays are written in silence.

Ah! We have action. The essay-writer is reaching for a pen!

If the camera zooms in now to the page, we can see a question has been written… "Show how the writer presents an atmosphere of violence in the story of Little Red Riding Hood." Look how the words "how", "atmosphere" and "'violence" have been underlined. The essay-writer puts down its pen, scratches its head, then picks up the pen.

Yes. Something is definitely happening. The essay-writer is making a list.

- the wolf eats Grandma
- the wolf eats Hood
- the wolf has big eyes, teeth, which are threatening
- Hood is dressed in red - colour of blood
- writer uses violent words like "seized", "chased", "mauled"
- the sky is described as "blood-red" - atmospheric
- Hood's mother puts in the basket for Grandma a bloodstained hatchet
- Hood stamps on an unwary insect on her way through the woods

The lesser spotted essay-writer looks content. Notice how it reaches for another biscuit as it reads through the list. What's it about to do now? It's picking up a book – *The Adventures of Little Red Riding Hood*. I think we're going to see *research* in action, if we're lucky. Yes! It's flicking through the pages of the book, looking to see if there are any more points it's missed. Now it's adding two more points.

- Hood has H.A.T.E. tattooed on her knuckles
- Grandma's living room has paintings of hunting scenes

The essay-writer pauses, and takes a thoughtful sip from a mug. Watch how it picks up its pen again. Notice the frown of concentration. Look! It's making marks against its original list. Ssshh!

Never before have we been so privileged as to see an essay-writer in action this close-up.

Let's zoom in further with the camera to see what's being written.

- *the wolf eats Grandma - incident p. 17*
- *the wolf eats Hood - incident p. 19*
- *the wolf has big eyes, teeth, which are threatening - descriptive detail p. 15*
- *Hood is dressed in red - colour of blood - descriptive detail pp. 1 & 3*
- *writer uses violent words like "seized", "chased", "mauled". - diction pp. 16-18*
- *the sky is described as blood-red - atmospheric - descriptive detail p. 4*
- *Hood's mother puts in the basket for Grandma a bloodstained hatchet - descriptive detail p. 5*
- *Hood stamps on an unwary insect on her way through the woods - descriptive detail p. 8*

- *Hood has H.A.T.E. tattooed on her knuckles - descriptive detail p. 5*
- *Grandma's living room has paintings of hunting scenes - descriptive detail p. 10.*

Three categories - incident, descriptive detail, diction, therefore three big paragraphs necessary...

How wonderful! We've just seen the essay-writer ORGANIZE its material into logical units called paragraphs. It's grouped all similar points together, therefore avoiding going through the whole story from the beginning to the end. Astonishing! Exquisite! We are truly privileged.

Of course, paragraphs are essential to any essay. They're generally around 12 to 15 sentences long. The first sentence of a paragraph starts a very little way in from the margin. The first sentence of a paragraph introduces the paragraph, and the last sums up and links the paragraph logically to the next and... Hold on! The essay-writer is beginning again. It eats another Jammy Dodger and is taking up its pen. It seems to be drawing. Is that a heart? With letters inside? "RJ 4 KR" Is this a strange essay-writing code? Fascinating!

Listen! The essay-writer is sighing now, and its eyes have taken on a dreamy look. Strange! We usually associate this behaviour with mating rituals, not essay-writing. Nevertheless, we have been lucky enough today to witness a superb example of planning an essay, including the brainstorming stage, the checking for extra points, and the organization into paragraphs. The essay-writer has been successfully selective in the points it made, avoiding the common error of just re-telling the story.

Sadly many lesser spotted essay-writers have become extinct through just re-telling the story or, worse still, just writing down everything they know. The examiners hide among the bulrushes and pick them out and shoot them down...

Well ... you won't get killed for just writing everything you can think of, but you won't get the grade you want. Plan to put in your essay only relevant points that answer the question.

Part two – The Ps and Qs of essay writing
P for paragraphs, and Q for quotations, that is.

a) Paragraphs
We've already seen how paragraphs are the vital building blocks of any kind of essay. But what do you put in them?

Since paragraphs generally explore one major point, they

should be composed of lots of small points plus evidence. There is a pattern you can use to help you fill out your paragraphs:

Point
Evidence
Explanation

or P-E-E for short. So, in order to write a first-class essay, you need to pee all over the paper.

Say you were writing an essay on the pressures facing teenagers:

A *point* might be: banning exams would reduce stress on teenagers.

The *evidence* might be: last year in a group of 50 teenagers taking exams, 45 of them regularly shouted at family members.

The *explanation* might be: these outbreaks of bad temper are obviously stress-related, and banning exams would help reduce tension in all families with teenagers.

Or maybe you're writing an essay about a character in a poem.

The *point* might be: he is timid.

The *evidence* might be: when "the clock struck one" the poet tells us, "the mouse ran down".

The *explanation* might be: therefore we can see the mouse is afraid of loud noises such as the clock striking, and his headlong rush back to the safety of the mousehole shows us his nervous nature.

Sometimes in an essay you might want to put two or three pieces of evidence down before making a comment on all of them together. Just remember, a point without evidence is useless. In a court of law, a barrister would not win a case if he or she just said, I think the defendant is guilty, so there! Proof must be given.

The same applies to you – if you wanted to prove to your dad it was your younger sister who was on the phone all the time and not you, you'd wait until she was on the phone, and take your dad in to catch her red-handed.

A cheering thought! If you write a literature essay and your ideas aren't shared exactly by the examiner, you'll still get credit for what you've written if you use point – evidence – explanation. It's rather like Maths, when if you answer a problem with the right method, you'll get some marks even if you end up with the wrong answer.

b) Quotations

Often for your evidence you'll want to *quote* from the text.

I'm glad you mentioned that. I never know how to set quotes out.

To be accurate for a moment, you should say "'quotations". "Quotation" is a noun and "to quote" is a verb.

Fussy, aren't you?

So are examiners. Anyway, here's the lowdown on using quotations.

1. **Always use quotation marks.**
If you don't, it looks as if you're just copying from the text, which is a big no-no. Using quotation marks means you're admitting you didn't make them up yourself!

2. **Keep quotations short.**
There's absolutely no point in copying out huge chunks of the text, especially if there's only a little bit of it that backs up your point. Quotations from novels shouldn't be much longer than one sentence, and often just a phrase is effective. Two to three lines of playscript or poetry is a good maximum limit.

3. **Make the quotation fit your sentence.**
For example…

> In <u>The Alternative Guide to GCSE English Language</u> the writer advises us to, "make the quotation fit your sentence".

If there's no main verb in the bit you're quoting, you'll need it in your part of the sentence.

4. **Always link your quotation to the point you're making –
don't leave it all by itself.**
E.g. Write…

> Spiders need to keep up with weather predictions. When we learn that the rain "washed the spider out" we feel pity laced with contempt for Incy-Wincy who should have been better prepared.

Don't write…

> Spiders need to keep up with weather predictions. "The rain came down and washed the spider out."

173

There is no logical connection between those last two sentences. The examiner would have to guess what you mean.

5. Take time choosing the part of the quotation that matters.
If you choose the wrong bit, you'll sound silly.
In a famous part of MACBETH, Macbeth says,

> **"Is this a dagger which I see before me
> The handle toward my hand?"**

Don't write:

> **When Macbeth is about to kill the king he
> hallucinates and sees "the handle toward my hand."**

This gives the impression he's terrified of doors.

6. If you're quoting lines from a poem or play, indent them and set them out apart from the rest of your writing.
Like this...

> **The stanza ends on a note of despairing finality:
> "All the king's horses and all the king's men
> Couldn't put Humpty together again."
> The repetition of the word "king" emphasizes how
> not even the highest person in the land could repair
> the shattered hero of this moving poem.**

Notice you don't need to leave any lines in-between.

Part three – writing your essay
When you've read the question, researched, then organized your answer, you're ready to start writing.

174

At last!

a) The Introduction

The introduction is possibly the most important and difficult part of writing an essay. Important because it's the first impression the reader gets of your essay, and difficult because it's *so* important you sometimes end up getting stage fright!

Just forget about essay writing for a moment and imagine this.

You're at a party with all your mates, and it's OK, but you know everyone and it's just the same old scene. Suddenly you see someone you've never met before, someone impossibly attractive, someone you just have to get to know – and quick, before anyone else does.

You nudge your best mate to point this person out.

"Oh, yeah," says your mate. "I know them. D'you want me to introduce you?"

You nod eagerly. But can you trust your mate to give a good impression of you?

You get taken up to this wonderful person you'd spotted. Your mate begins the intro.

"Hi, this is (insert your name!). He (or she) was born in 1986 in a small village outside the town, although (his or her) parents moved into town three years later. The family lives in a small semi-detached house near the shops. She (or he) attends the local comprehensive school and…"

Meanwhile two more people approach the gorgeous person. One of them begins, "Hi. This is my mate. He (or she) is sixteen, and would like to get to know you better. I'll leave you to it, shall I?"

You beat up your mate while the gorgeous person starts chatting to your competitor.

Lesson learnt? Introductions should be brief, direct and powerful.

Applying this to essays, you should:

- Mention the **subject** you're writing about in the first sentence (it could be a text or texts).

- **Re-phrase** the question or title in your own words to show you understand what you're doing.

- **Hint** at how your essay will proceed, and provide a link to the second paragraph. (Links are vital to the flow and logic of your essay.)

Like this:

Essay question:
Are teenagers better off living in the city or in the country?

Your introduction:
There are good and bad points about living in both the city and country. For teenagers there are special reasons why one might be better than the other. Teenagers like a good social life, shops, cinemas, sports facilities, clubs and places to go. Can you get these in both the city and the country?

This intro works quite well because we can see that the writer has addressed the question, and also we guess he or she will go on to look at the provision of the facilities listed. The readers feel as if they know where they're being taken.

IN EXAMS: Keep intros brief and don't agonize over them.
IN COURSEWORK: Write your intro out in rough first and fiddle around with it to get it right.

b) Essay style tips
Once your introduction's written, you've broken the ice and can get on with your essay.

Now we're on the subject of writing essays, I've got some questions.

Fire away.

177

I don't want to be awkward here, but that depends on a lot of factors. You'd expect a coursework essay to be longer than an exam essay because of the time factor, and an essay on one short poem would be shorter than an essay on a whole Shakespeare play. But generally three or four paragraphs is too short for an essay, and eight sides of A4 paper in normal-sized handwriting is getting on to be too long. More than twelve sides and you could bore for Britain.

No. Write in plain English. But don't use slang, either. Look at these three examples from a literature essay on *Jane Eyre*, and pick the one you think is best:

a) Jane Eyre is one cool chick. Like I say, she sorted out that John Reed when he chucked the book at her. Mind you, he deserved it, what with him calling her names and making out he was a big shot. Like Jane is caring and nice really, but you can't blame her for losing her rag completely!

b) Jane Eyre, the eponymous heroine of the novel of that name, is a trenchant and incisive character. On being inexorably oppressed by the juvenile John Reed, who delivered the projectile of a book at her cranium, she irrupted upon him, despite her natural benevolence, because she was provoked beyond her circumscription.

c) Jane is not afraid to stand up for herself. At the beginning of the novel she attacks John Reed when he throws a book at her head. She does this in the heat of the moment as she cannot stand his bullying behaviour any longer.

a) Sounds fun to chat to, but hasn't written a successful paragraph. Formal essays should never contain slang unless it's in quoted dialogue, and should avoid vague words such as "caring", "nice" and "really".

b) Has swallowed a dictionary! The paragraph doesn't make sense, even though it seems to sound good at first. This writing is just as bad as **a)**. Remember, if you don't understand what you have written, no one else will.

c) Is most definitely the best of the three. The English is clear and straightforward and uncluttered. Even if you haven't read the book that's being written about, you can understand the paragraph. That's the test of a first-class essay.

179

Point taken. But I still feel I need help with my essay writing.

Then read this:

The Agony Aunt,
Saccharine Magazine,
Queen's Yard,
London

Dear Mandy,

Yesterday I was kept in for detention and I watched my English teacher marking my essay. First she ticked it in a few places, then less frequently, and then I stared as her eyes grew heavy and her head nodded forward on to the page. Once she began to snore gently we all tip-toed out. My mates said I was ace for writing such a boring essay, but this is the eleventh time this has happened. What's wrong with me?

Louise

> Dear Louise,
>
> I was so touched by your letter that the editor and I have invited your essay to London for the day to have a complete makeover by our style experts!

Before

Jane Eyre is kind. We know this because she is kind to Adele. Jane Eyre gets angry. We know this because she fights with John Reed. Jane Eyre likes reading. We know this because we see her reading a book. Jane Eyre is loving. We know this because she likes Bessie. Jane Eyre is frightened of ghosts. We know this because she is frightened of a ghost. It says, "Miss Jane screamed so loud." She screamed so loud because she was frightened of a ghost. This shows she is frightened of ghosts. "I thought a ghost would come." This also shows she is frightened of ghosts ... sss ... zzzz.

During – our experts get to work:

"The trouble with Louise's essay is that she repeats herself – a big fashion mistake, as bad as wearing hot pants over your jeans. When I start the makeover I'm going to get rid of all the repetitions."
Priscilla Purple,
colour consultant

Priscilla Purple.

"Louise's sentences are all the same length. This is why her readers keep falling asleep – they're being hypnotized. I'm going to get to work on Louise's sentence structure to break things up a bit."
Giovanni Mantovani,
fashion guru

"I sympathize with Louise because it's hard to know what phrase to use to link your point, evidence and explanation. I'm going to take her essay to my studio in Docklands where she can choose from a mind-blowing selection of linking words and phrases."
Dana De Ville,
designer

"Louise's essay doesn't sound as if it's enjoying itself very much. She's got to hint at some enthusiasm, some sense that the essay is worth writing. Her language needs to be more exciting."
Gloria Freud-Young,
therapist

After

Jane Eyre has a fascinating character because it isn't always simple. She certainly has a kind side; this is suggested by her thoughtful treatment of Adele, her pupil, and the way she is happy to receive Bessie's attention. She is very sensitive, too. Jane is forced to stay in the Red Room where she thinks she sees a ghost. Bessie's words, "Miss Jane screamed so loud" imply how terrified she must have been. Yet Jane is also capable of physical bravery. When the bully John Reed throws a book at her and then pulls her hair, she flies at him and fights back.

Well, Louise, how do you feel now?

Wonderful! My essay is lively and interesting. When I gave it to my teacher to read she sat up, smiled, ticked it over and over again, punched the air and cried, Yesss!!

You too can improve your essays with the following useful phrases.

Don't just say "this shows", try...

implies	suggests
hints	gives the impression
conveys the idea	indicates
is evidence	tells us

You never need use the same word twice again!

In a literature coursework essay if you want to say a character is, for example, evil, and you don't want to keep using the word "evil", here's something to try to help you expand your vocabulary – the word spidergram.

Put the word "evil" in the middle of a piece of paper and see how many other words you can come up with that have virtually the same meaning. You could even do this with a friend, and compare scores.

malicious

live backwards (only joking)

nasty

EVIL

mean

wicked!

demonic

monstrous

diabolic

184

Now you have a fund of words you can use during your essay.

WARNING

If you use a thesaurus (sort of dictionary that lists words which have similar meanings to other words) treat it with caution. Only use words with which you are already familiar, otherwise you might misuse a word, or misapply it.

c) The conclusion

Funny how you get a finishing spurt towards the end of an essay. Just don't put on such a spurt that you forget about the conclusion.

185

You need a conclusion to round off your essay and answer the question in the title once and for all.

A conclusion should:
- Briefly recall the major points you have made.
- Point out again how these address the question or fulfil the task.
- Finish with a sentence that sounds really final.

Here's a sample conclusion:

Essay question:
Are teenagers better off living in the city or in the country?

Your introduction:
For most teenagers, city life seems more appealing, because there are more shops, clubs, leisure facilities and generally more things to do. However, for teenagers who enjoy walking, open spaces, or who have many friends in the country, the country is probably best. So a minority of teenagers will always prefer the country – provided there is a town nearby.

This conclusion answers the question once and for all, and the final sentence sounds as if it is a final sentence. Remember the conclusion is the last thing your reader reads, and you want to leave a good impression. You don't want to do the equivalent of walking out of a room and falling flat on your face...

But now you've finished reading this section, you won't!

Orals make me want to scream!

Every English GCSE includes an oral component – that means (in plain English) that you'll get a certain amount of marks for how well you talk.

Brilliant, eh?

Unfortunately this does not mean how well you:

- imitate all your favourite sitcom characters
- stay on the phone all evening
- cheer and jeer at matches
- chat up the opposite sex
- get your own way when it comes to deciding what to watch on telly.

It *does* mean whether you can...

explain – describe – narrate...
explore – analyse – imagine...
discuss – argue – persuade...

And your English teacher has to be around to hear you do it. This means oral exercises have to be assessed in the classroom. It's up to you whether you believe the story of the student who was so shy that his English teacher couldn't get a word out of him. Not to be defeated, when he saw the boy in town one evening he stopped him and asked him directions to the football ground. The boy was clear, accurate and polite. The teacher counted it as an oral assignment.

You probably won't be so lucky.

You'll be expected to perform a number of different oral assignments, to show you can:

- communicate facts in a direct manner
- talk in order to solve problems and co-operate with others
- use language to persuade.

This is not so different from written English, except you talk. And quite often, everyone in the class is watching you talk. Some particularly sadistic English teachers might video you, but none of them has won an Oscar yet...

I bet you really look forward to oral assignments, don't you?

DEBBIE: No way – I get really embarrassed. I hate it when I think everybody's looking at me.

NEELAM: I worry that my words are going to come out wrong.

PAUL: Yeah, and all your mates will think you're boring or stupid.

JON: I think it's the best part of the course. I like standing in front of the class and sounding off. Talking's a lot easier than writing.

NEELAM: Yeah, but that's as long as people are smiling at you. Then it gives you a confidence boost. But if they don't – panic!

PAUL: Yeah. I gave a talk about the monarchy once and everyone ended up having a go at me.

So come on, tell us, have your orals ever turned into total disasters?

NEELAM :   I hate it when you run out of things to say and the teacher's grinning at you, waiting for you to carry on.

189

DEBBIE: What's worse is when everyone laughs and what you're saying isn't meant to be funny.

PAUL: Or when you dry up completely.

DEBBIE: That happened to me once. I just wanted to die.

JON: That's nothing. In the middle of my GCSE talk, the fire-alarm went off.

Do you prefer group work or pair work to talking alone?

JON: You don't get as stressed if you're working with your mates, but if you get a good idea and everybody else disagrees, it can really get to you. The idea carries on developing in your head and you get more and more frustrated.

NEELAM: We usually end up arguing all the time.

DEBBIE: We do lots of group work in our class. Once we had to decide on the meaning of this poem, and it was really hard. So Leanne told us about her latest boyfriend instead and when the teacher came over we hadn't done anything.

PAUL: Yeah, group work's a doss until the teacher comes over.

DEBBIE: Yeah, you have to sound dead intelligent.

PAUL: Me, I just shut up when I know the teacher's listening.

Have you got any good tips for first-timers?

PAUL: If you suffer from nerves, just imagine you're talking to one person, your mate, or something.

JON: If you've got to say something in front of the class, have it all planned out, with notes you can glance at, in case you dry up.

DEBBIE: Yeah, but if you just read your notes it can be boring. You're only supposed to use them as a prompt.

NEELAM: And don't be so nervous that you talk in a whisper – you've got to get people to hear you after all your hard work!

JON: And you have to look at your audience, not at your shoes.

DEBBIE: And whatever you do, don't get the giggles.

Nightmare scenarios ... aargh!

1. You begin to deliver your perfectly rehearsed and accentuated talk. Everyone's face is blank. This is because they cannot hear a word...

AVOID by remembering that if you are speaking in front of an audience it's always necessary to raise your voice. Practise at home by standing at the top of the stairs and proclaiming to someone at the bottom. (Tough if you've got a flat – improvise!)

2. Younormallytalkveryfastbecauseit'scoolhey?andyouhavesuch alottosayandyouwanttogetitoveranddonewith ... but if you gabble, no one will be able to make out what you're saying.

AVOID by taking a chill pill. Nice 'n' slowly does it. Take a deep breath before you begin, pause occasionally and keep remembering to breathe!

3. You start your talk, and your mates are nodding appreciatively. Your teacher, however, looks utterly baffled. He doesn't understand a word you say.

AVOID by not letting your speech get too influenced by the latest American comedy show or street talk. The art of doing well at GCSE oral is to make your language fit your audience and purpose. If the situation is meant to be formal, talk formally – but there's no need to sound posh, unless you have to pretend you're at an ambassador's garden party.

4. You start your talk. It's going well. It's a bit tiring being on your feet for so long, so you slouch against the blackboard. Not near a blackboard? You lean on the desk. Or sit down, and put your feet on the desk… There are horrified looks from the teacher.

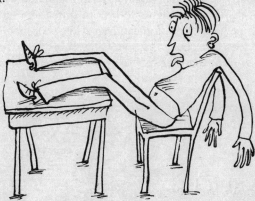

AVOID by remembering that a good posture matters when addressing an audience. Remain on your feet and look as if you mean business – otherwise your audience will quickly lose interest.

5. Talking to the class like this makes you feel a bit nervous. So you toss back your hair. It falls forward, so you toss it back again. You twiddle your ear. Hmm, nice! You twiddle your ear again. You toss back your hair, twiddle your ear, click your knuckles, toss back your hair – don't you just hate speakers with irritating habits?

AVOID by finding out what your irritating habits are. Check them out with a good friend. Then stand with your hands held together behind you, or tie your hair back – but only if your habits really annoy. Don't turn yourself into a zombie. Similarly you might have irritating verbal habits such as saying, *like*, every so often, or, *stuff like that*. Don't overdo them, and go easy on the '*um*'s and '*er*'s.

6. Your talk is about to begin. On the blackboard you stick up a huge map you've brought with you of the main transport routes into your town. Sigh of appreciation from English teacher impressed at your degree of preparation. You then get out your video of the Number 37 bus route, and wink at your mate sitting by the lights so he can turn them off and your multi-media presentation can begin. But your mate is asleep. The video turns out to be your younger brother's Teletubbies tape, and the map begins to slip down from the blackboard...

AVOID by keeping preparations for oral assignments simple. The more complicated it gets, the more things there are to go wrong. Never use a video unless you're going to discuss what you're showing, and even then, keep it brief. Ideally, a talk should be just you and your notes.

7. You are about to start your talk. You look out on the faces of your classmates. Omigod, this is awful! There you are, all on your tod, and there they are – what are they thinking of you? – is your hair OK? – and what was it you were going to say? You go scarlet, and wish the earth would swallow you up.

AVOID stage-fright by pretending you are someone else. This sounds crazy, but it works. It's a well-known fact that the second most common fear is speaking in public, so virtually everyone suffers from speaker's nerves. (The first is illness.) This fear is activated when you become conscious of what you are doing – i.e. self-conscious. So try to think of yourself as someone else. Or imagine you're giving a talk on behalf of someone else. Or that you've been bribed, heavily, not to be nervous. Or, even better, get your parents to bribe you, heavily, not to be nervous. That should do it.

What if you have a strong accent?
Don't worry. Accents never count against you. Provided you can be easily understood by people in your area, you're OK. Be proud of who you are!

Talking to an audience
Learn these five tricks:

1. Use notes
NEVER read a speech. This is not giving a talk – it's reading aloud, and thus a wholly different activity. Plus, if you are reading, you're not looking at the audience, and their feelings are hurt. (Well … maybe not … but they do want to see your face!)

Instead, get into the habit of making brief notes, preferably with bullet points of your main ideas, on cards *not* A4 sheets of paper, so that you don't forget what to say. Practise using notes so that you don't get lost. Experienced speakers tag cards together in case they fall on the floor and scatter!

2. Use body language
If all the audience has got to look at is you, make yourself look interesting. (No, I'm not suggesting fake lashes!) Watch actors on TV or on the stage – you never catch them just standing stock still. Use your hands to emphasise a point, make an occasional gesture, or even move around a bit, but not too much.

Relax, and remember to change your tone of voice occasionally. Create variety. A dull monotone is only effective if you're training to be a hypnotherapist.

3. Keep contact with your audience

Do this with your eyes. Divide the audience into three sections – left, middle, right. Find one friendly face in each section. Take it in turns to direct your speech to them. And *smile*!

4. Keep it simple

Audiences can't take in a lot at one sitting. Just think what you feel like in a lesson where the teacher just drones on and on boring you rigid. Similarly, if your talk is too long, complicated, detailed, or full of statistics, your audience will nod off, and one by one fall off their seats with an annoying thump.

A good talk should be reasonably brief – ask your teacher how long you've got, but five to eight minutes is reasonable. Have a clear structure so that the audience knows where it is at any given time – either at the beginning, in the middle, or coming to the end. Another tip – it's not a good idea to pass visual props round the audience while you're talking. They'll be too interested in examining whatever's being passed round and they won't listen to you.

5. Use humour and drama

Spice up a talk with a joke or two – everyone loves jokes and they give the impression that you are confident.

Or try wringing the audience's heartstrings, perhaps by describing one suffering individual, so they feel desperately sorry for him. Use a specific example to bring the truth of what you are saying home to your audience.

We can work it out

Learning to talk in groups or pairs is just as important as talking alone to the class. In fact, it's likely that most of your oral work will be in groups or pairs. You might be asked to study a poem together, discuss an issue, decide how to run an imaginary campaign to combat homelessness, prepare an item for the school council – the list is endless. Here you aren't talking to an audience although it's quite likely that your teacher will creep up on you to eavesdrop and assess. You're supposed to ignore him or her although in practice it's impossible. Your teacher is hoping to find out how good you are at collaborative talking – that is, talking with others to reach a decision.

Here's a checklist of things you should try to do…

Listening

You'll get marked down if you don't listen to the others in your group. So pay attention to what everyone else says. Don't interrupt too often. Show your teacher you're listening by *looking* at the person who's talking, and then *picking up* on whatever they're saying and responding to it, i.e. by developing their point or offering a different perspective on the same idea.

Co-operating

If everyone else in your group has one idea, and you have another, you'll have to give way. In group work, majority decision rules OK. In pair work, opt for the great British compromise. Just sticking out for what you want won't impress anyone.

Leading
Someone has to direct a group discussion and from time to time this might be you. Good leaders aren't bossy, and in fact make it their job to check that everyone's opinions are taken into account. They then sum up, state the group decision, and move the discussion on. They give the quiet members of the group the space to have their say. They don't overrule everyone to get their plans carried through – it's a good oral GCSE mark you're after, not world domination.

Re-stating
If someone says something that isn't clear to you, re-state it in your own words, and check you've got it right. For example, say, *Are you saying that...?* This is a good way of taking part in discussions without necessarily having any ideas of your own!

Asking questions
Be prepared to ask the group members questions about their views. This is a very friendly thing to do as it helps them score points. Also their ideas might give you some ideas.

Choosing to be polite
Although your best mate *will* finally agree with you if you pin her to the floor and extract her teeth one by one, your English teacher will be distinctly underwhelmed. Instead, express your opinions with consideration for others, and use phrases that are modest-sounding, e.g.

> **Well, I think that...**
> **Yes, but it seems to me that...**
> **I understand what you're saying, but...**

Saying enough
One great temptation in group or pair work is to let someone else do all the talking. Big mistake. If your teacher doesn't hear you say

anything, how can he or she mark you? If you're in a group with the loudmouths of the class, make sure you get a word in. Supergluing their mouths shut isn't really advisable, but keep on in there until they listen to you, and don't feel you have to let people interrupt you.

For guidance on how to be persistent in an argument, tune in to a talk radio station, either a local or national one. Listen to politicians arguing, and nab some of their phrases.

Which words do you use?

Talking isn't that much different from writing, in that you make your language suit your purpose.

Generally, in oral work, use plain, straightforward English. If your activity involves a literary subject, such as discussing a book, use the language that goes with that activity (*simile, metaphor, atmosphere* – see page 120). If you are giving a speech persuading people to change their minds on an issue, use persuasive language.

I beg you, ladies and gentlemen, just think for a moment about the plight of the Ruritanian refugee...

If you are asked to do a role-play and have to pretend to be someone else, talk in the way they would – as long as you can still talk effectively. If your teacher asks you to be Napoleon, the pig from *Animal Farm*, you're not supposed to just go, "Oink, oink"!

201

I'll just hide until the exams are over!

Which do you prefer – coursework or exams?

Definitely coursework. Exams scare the hell out of me.

Coursework bugs me. I hate the way it hangs over you. The good thing about exams is that they're over quickly.

If you get stuck on your coursework folder you can see the teacher. You can't ask for help in exams – worst luck.

I'm not that brilliant at English, but I seem to do better in exams. I think it's the stress – a bit like before an important match.

I can hack coursework, but I lose it in exams. It's the time thing. It takes me ages to get started, and then I never finish.

I always end up leaving my coursework to the last minute and the teacher goes mental because I hand it in late.

Your coursework folder

Always make sure you're clear about the number of pieces that are supposed to be in your coursework folder, what they should consist of, and when the whole folder should be complete. If you know what you're aiming towards, it makes you feel more in control.

Coursework must be your own work. Not your mum's, not your aunty Joan's, and not copied out of a book. You've got to sign a cover sheet to show your work is original.

Have one piece written in your own handwriting. Some boards insist on this, as it proves you really did the work. Some of your folder can be word-processed, but you will have to say if you used a spell-check facility.

Generally teachers will help you spread out the work for your coursework essays by telling you how many homeworks to spend on it. They might give you lesson time too. Don't be tempted either to leave it all to the last minute, *or* to ignore all your other work in an attempt to write the best coursework essay in the world ever – you can't get more than 20/20!

However, because you can spend longer on coursework than on an exam question, you do have the opportunity to write a first draft.

Drafting

Basically, making a first attempt at your coursework, then getting feedback, and using the feedback to write the final version.

Sometimes a second version will get you a much better mark. Also feedback comments can help you improve all of your English. Famous writers have been known to rewrite their 400 page novels over and over again. And you're complaining about one piece of coursework!

Hmmm ... What does this drafting process entail?

1. Write your first attempt.

2. Read it through and see where you think you could have done better.

3. Give it to your teacher and get comments from him or her.

4. Rewrite the piece of work changing it according to the teacher's suggestions.

But I don't usually read the teacher's comments. I just look at the mark at the bottom.

Now you're doing GCSE you should get into the habit of looking carefully at the comment. It's there to help you. Just as you'd listen to your team's coach analyse your performance after a match, or your mate's comments about what you're wearing, take on board what your teacher tells you.

When you get feedback, it's very important that you shouldn't hear it as adverse criticism. It most definitely isn't. Your teacher is taking time to give you advice on how to improve your work.

Yeah, but it's hard seeing how you could have done something differently. And I can't stand it when the teacher tells me a whole page I've written is useless and I have to lose it.

I sympathize. But T. S. Eliot, one of the twentieth century's greatest poets, spent around four *years* writing his poem, "The Waste Land". Then he sent it to his poet friend Ezra Pound to read and give him his comments. Ezra told T. S. Eliot to cut the poem by about four-fifths! He took the advice, they remained friends, and the poem is now world-famous.

Using your teacher's comments

1. Speak to your teacher if you're not clear what you've been told.

2. Think about the teacher's comments and write them down somewhere in your own words.

3. Decide whether your first draft only needs minor alterations in places, or whether you need to rewrite the whole piece. Your teacher will help you decide. (But don't throw away that first draft – it might come in useful.)

Some English GCSE candidates get quite fond of their coursework folders, and can hardly bear to give them up to the examiner for marking.

If that's you, you'll be delighted to know you can usually get your coursework folder back after GCSE grades have been awarded. You can then get it framed and decorate your bedroom with it.

Examinations

Whether they're for English or a medical, examinations bring everyone out into a cold sweat – so you're not alone! Maybe it's something about that enforced silence, the scratching of pens on paper, the steely glare of the invigilator... Help! I can't take it any more!

However, exams needn't be a nightmare if you're properly prepared – psychologically as well as in practical terms.

No. By "psychologically", I mean it's just a matter of getting exams into proportion. They're only written tests to see what standard you've reached – they shouldn't be the be-all and end-all of your existence.

If your parents are bribing you to do well by offering to buy you something if you get a certain grade, refuse it –

– and ask for the reward for trying your best *instead*. You don't want to feel scared of failure – that won't help at all.

TOP TIP
Don't moan to your mates about how dreadful exams are. The more you wind each other up, the more you'll dread the exams. Find other things to talk about and don't let exams take over.

Apart from psychological preparation, there are other ways you should prepare yourself for your final encounter with the examiner.

The seven pillars of wisdom

1. Read this book again – it'll refresh your memory on those vital skills.

2. Look over your old work to find the errors you're prone to. Make sure you know why you made those mistakes, and also how to avoid them.

3. Pay attention – a lot of it! – when you go over old exam papers in class. Your English teacher will give you loads of last minute tips.

4. Grab a look at as many recent old exam papers as possible. Exam boards have an annoying habit of changing the layout of the papers or the kinds of questions they ask. The more familiar you are with the wording of a range of past questions, the clearer you'll be on what exactly you'll be expected to do in *your* exam.

5. If you have an anthology that you are being tested on, spend time studying and familiarizing yourself with the contents. The better you know it, the more confident you'll be.

6. In the run-up to the exam, become sensitive to written English by reading the newspapers and reading some good books. Note any words you didn't know before, find out what they mean, and resolve to use them.

7. Make sure you are absolutely clear about what you are going to be asked to do in the exam – and even what days the different papers are on! Remind yourself how much time you'll have for each question.

The night before

Provided you have followed the seven pillars of wisdom above, here are some helpful suggestions for the night before your English exam.

1. Watch your fave programmes on TV.
2. Listen to your latest CD.
3. Make a round of toast and eat it dripping with butter.
4. Go to bed early.
5. Er … that's it.

The most helpful thing you can have in the morning is a clear head. Oh, and a pen that isn't about to run out of ink. Working late on the night before an important exam is always a bad idea. Sleep refreshes you. So just relax…

And let's hope you don't resemble any of the following exam candidates…

Laidback Lewis

...who strolls whistling into the exam hall, not a
care in the world, runs a comb through his
hair, winks confidently at his mates,
turns over the examination paper, and
discovers it isn't English after all,
but Biology...

Distracting Deb

...who, once the exam starts, knocks over her bag of sweets,
forcing the invigilator to come over and pick them up, then
drops her ruler with a clatter, prompting another trip by the
invigilator. Then her chair squeaks as she rocks back and
forth on it, and after a fit
of sniffing she flings her
hand up to ask
the invigilator
for a tissue,
and wallops
the poor soul
who's sitting
behind her...

Neurotic Neil

...who hasn't slept a wink all night
hallucinating about the paper, and comes in
from the school toilets where he's been all
morning, clutching his bottle of Rescue
Remedy and his lucky mascot, repeating to
himself over and over again the list of
spellings he's been playing to himself
on his Walkman all week. Then he
turns over the paper, takes ten
calming breaths, and the invigilator
rushes over, convinced he's having an asthma attack...

211

Dithering Danny

...who turns over the exam paper, reads it through, reads it through again, thinks very, very carefully about which questions to answer, then how to answer them, then wonders if that really is the best way to answer them, then wonders whether it's a good idea to spend all this time wondering about how to answer the questions, and then wonders...

Got-the-Gear Graeme

...who comes with all the right equipment – three brand-new biros, pencils in case the biros run out, his new sports watch which tells the time in Outer Mongolia, two rubbers, a pencil sharpener, a packet of mints, state of the art trainers. Then when the exam begins he works out exactly how long he's got on his designer calculator, admires his trainers, tests each of his pens, then glances at the clock and sees there's only half an hour to go...

Caffeine Caryn

...who didn't sleep last night because she decided to leave all her preparation until bedtime, had a mug of coffee on the hour every hour, was still wide awake at six this morning. Then she sits down at her desk, turns over the paper, thinks how pretty the words look dancing on the page, studies the picture that goes with the creative writing question, imagines how nice it would be to be curled up in a corner of that Alpine meadow, and drifts happily off to sleep…

Enthusiastic Emma

…who is absolutely thrilled to discover that she can do – she really can do! – the first comprehension question (it's so easy) and proceeds to write down every little thing she possibly can to show the examiner that she can answer the question, and writes and writes and writes and writes and the invigilator calls time and she's only answered the one question…

Intimidating Ian

…who strides purposefully into the exam hall, assembles his armoury of pens, gets straight down to work, writing reams and reams, constantly puts his hand up to ask for more paper, wipes his forehead to demonstrate the huge mental effort he's making, gives in a script for marking twice as thick as anybody else's – lucky they know how huge his handwriting is, otherwise his mates'd be really worried…

Or perhaps you're just like the rest of us who are naturally terrified to begin with, fight a slight panic attack, but buckle down to work, keeping an eye on the clock, are amazed at how quickly the time goes. Before you know it, the whole thing is over (yesss!) and you're out again in the fresh air.

REMEMBER – if you have a genuine problem, such as dyslexia, or a tendency to panic severely in exams, special provisions can be made for you. Check your teacher knows if you fall into these categories well before the exam.

Exam battleplan

1. (This one's easy.) Turn over your paper.

2. In exams, *timing is everything*! Start by working out exactly how long you've got for each question. Remember to build in reading time. Jot down somewhere exactly what time to start each sub-section so you've got a personal timetable in front of you, e.g.

> 9.30 – 10.00 section A first qn
> 10.00 –10.30 section A second qn
> 10.30 –11.30 section B

Most exam papers these days tell you how long to spend on each question.

Whatever you do, stick to your timetable – it's crazy to throw away marks just because you haven't had time to answer a question that you knew the answer to!

3. Choose the right questions. In English exams, you might be given a choice of tasks. How do you know which one is right for you? Try to choose questions that you find interesting or familiar and which spark off lots of thoughts. Avoid questions that make your mind go blank or which you don't feel you understand.

Make a preliminary choice as to which question you're going to do. It doesn't matter if you change your mind *before* you settle down to your choice – just try not to change your mind halfway through!

4. Check you're about to answer the correct number of questions. If the paper offers you either question a) or question b) you won't get extra marks for tackling both – the frightening truth is that your answer for b)

will be ignored completely – think of all that hard work gone to waste!

5. If there's a passage-based question, remember to read the passage very carefully.

6. Make sure you read all the questions carefully, double-checking you're about to do exactly what is asked. NONE of these preparations for answering the questions are a waste of time. In fact they are vital to guarantee success.

7. Begin writing. If your arm hurts, flex your elbow several times, but be careful not to splatter the person next to you with ink. Make sure your writing isn't so untidy that it's illegible. Use a slow pen if you have messy handwriting (i.e. an ink or rollerball pen, not a ballpoint pen).

8. If you come across something you don't understand, especially in a comprehension, don't feel obliged to use it in your answer. You should be able to write a good answer without it. Just ignore it.

9. If you lose confidence in what you're writing, realizing you've misunderstood the passage or the question, pause. Is it just you being nervous, or have you really messed up? If you have messed up (and nobody's perfect) put a single line through your work and start again, being as concise as possible.

10. When you've finished a question, move on. Don't keep fretting about what you've written. It's done now, and it was the best you could do at the time. If you run over time trying to improve it, you'll only gain two or

three extra marks. The trouble is, you risk not having time to answer the next question. Even an average attempt at the next question might get you, say, twelve marks. So even though it's English, think mathematically. You haven't the time in an exam to be a perfectionist.

11. If you finish before time don't amuse yourself by asking to go to the toilet every five minutes or catching up with your beauty sleep – re-read the questions and your answers looking particularly at spelling, grammar and paragraphing. And check you've answered absolutely every part of all the questions you've chosen.

12. Try to finish slightly before time is called, so you do have time for a quick check and read-through and opportunity to make any last-minute corrections. Give yourself a mental pat on the back for having done so well. And it's all over…

Not exactly. You can never escape from English. It's there. All around you. Everywhere you go, it's on billboards, posters –

Precisely. People talk to you in it all the time. If you want to get away from English completely, your only hope is to emigrate to a remote South Sea island where everyone speaks Tagalog.

Has studying English really been that bad?

There's always English Language A-Level.

Answers

Even basics drive me batty!
Page 29
there, too, whether, principle, their, weather, two, two, to, lose, too, they're.

Page 41
Possible answers:
1. ...
2. ;
3. ( )
4. –

Hands up who hates comprehension?
Page 68
1. "This pro-hormone with its added ingredient of selenio-zirconium"
2. 999/1000 people
3. Hollywood superstars, chart-topping boy bands
4. "the once-over", "what is it with you?", "fancy", "babes", "blokes", "drop-dead gorgeous", "gals", "copoff", "pulling", "crazy love life"
5. "the magic ingredient with the ultimate pulling power"
6. the scene at the club, the pensioner

Page 86
Here are some points you may have picked up:

Paragraph one
- Kicks off with a description of an imaginary manhole cover attack.
- Uses the second person (you) to make it immediate, to make *you* feel as if it's happening to you.
- Contrasts "enjoying a quiet drink" with "a deafening explosion", therefore shocking you.
- Uses dramatic words and phrases to describe the incident – "deafening", "a column of flame *leaps* into the air", "hurtling", "vicious", "exploding".

Paragraph two
- Points out that an exploding manhole cover could kill you – "potentially lethal".

Paragraph three
- Chooses to let an eye-witness do the talking, so we identify with him.
- Includes his name, age and job, so he seems real to us – if it happened to him, it could happen to us (shock! horror!).
- He also uses dramatic words and phrases, e.g. "this massive explosion", "incredibly loud and sinister buzzing sound", "total shock and panic", "children were crying", etc., etc.

Paragraph four
- The writer chooses to describe all the horrific injuries suffered by the bystanders, e.g. "first and second degree burns".
- Allows Raffaella Galasso to give first hand account and in…

Paragraph five
- She goes on to describe in detail how it affected her life afterwards – "even now taking a tube or getting a lift makes me nervous".

Paragraph six
  (Just the causes – nothing very relevant here – and we've used this paragraph already.)

Paragraph seven
– The writer says the *Big Issue* has learned of *at least* three incidents ... in London *alone* – making it sound as if there were more than three, and they might be happening all over the country – many accidents just waiting to happen!

Paragraph eight
– The episodes are described as "alarming" (an emotive word) and as "worldwide" (wherever you go, there's no escape!).

Paragraph nine
– Joe McNally suggests there's a mystery here – "it's a very odd story". He almost gives the impression there's a worldwide conspiracy.

Paragraph ten
– Manhole covers are described as "potential death traps" – strong, emotive language, and the thought that they are there is "not a comforting one", i.e. we can't take a walk in safety any more!
– Describing Mark Woodward as a "survivor" suggests he could have been killed.

Paragraph eleven
– Raffaella Galasso contrasts the "lovely sunny day" with the "nightmare" of the "most terrible experience" of her life.